Godly...But Gay

A Story of Contradictions, Conversion Therapy, & Coming Out

Godly...But Gay

A Story of Contradictions, Conversion Therapy,
& Coming Out

Joel Barrett

Kansas City, Missouri
www.joelspeaksout.com

Joel Barrett
Godly...But Gay
A Story of Contradictions, Conversion Therapy,
& Coming Out

Cover Photo: Emily Sexton
Author Photos: Emily Sexton & Aaron Burson

ISBN: 9798502400640

Printed in the United States of America

DEDICATION

To my husband David, who saw who I was becoming instead of who I was and loved me despite it all. David, you are still my BOFA (Breath Of Fresh Air).

No Reserves. No Retreats. No Regrets.

– William Borden

ACKNOWLEDGMENTS

Writing acknowledgements feels like one of those speeches at an awards show when the person tries to thank a long list of people before the music starts playing, meanwhile those of us watching are thinking "I don't care about this long list of meaningless names." So before the music starts playing I'd like to mention just a few names that may mean nothing to you, but they mean the world to me.

Natasha Ria El-Scari - my manuscript developer, editor, creative consultant, and friend. I now realize this book would have never been completed without you. I was drowning in a sea of words and ideas until you helped me find direction, clarity, purpose, and my voice. Natasha, I can't thank you enough.

Gloria (Swardenski) Kane - you have been my friend, confidant, sister, and coach for over thirty years. Can you believe that?! Thank you for always believing in me and loving me unconditionally.

Christopher Hooper - thank you for your Gay 101 classes and all the laughs, tears, and eye rolls.

Dr. Nicole Price - thank you for knocking on my door to see where the book is all these months...okay years... of me saying I'm writing a book. You are an inspiration.

Dr. April Lidinsky - your creative nonfiction writing class helped me see myself as a writer for the first time in my life. Thank you for your belief in me all these years.

My children Juliet, Shym, and Annemarie - You lived much of this story. You loved your dad in the midst of it all. We had some rough times and some fun times. We made it. I love you each so much and am proud to call you my children.

To everyone over the years who has said, "Wow, that's quite a story. You should write a book!" I did. Thank you for the encouragement.

FOREWORD

Throughout my life I have been paralyzed by a crisis of faith at various times where I felt I had to choose my faith or my sexuality. As life would have it, however, both were unalterably shaped by two very specific experiences that caused me to question myself — and my faith. For as long as I live, I will never forget either of the them.

"This hurts me more than you know." Those were the words of the senior pastor as he unceremoniously terminated me from employment at the several thousand member pentecostal church that had for several years been the center of my life. But I wasn't alone. My friend and eventual lover was fired too. I was 19. He was 24. We met two years prior at an evangelical Bible college in Tulsa, Oklahoma.

Before heading off to school that summer, my pastor warned me about the risk I was taking going to his alma mater. Spotting me dancing in church one day, he called over one of the other members of the ministerial staff to witness the conversation he wanted to have with me. "Be careful when you get down there," he said. "They'll pretend to want to help you all so that they can take advantage of you."

I was confused, embarrassed and completely demoralized in that moment. After all, I wondered, what was it about me expressing myself that would merit someone wanting to harm me? And, yet, I knew what he was intimating — and conflating. His clear belief was that gay people were predators and I would be their ideal prey. He could not have been more wrong. I was loved, supported and protected throughout my time there.

The other experience occurred several years later in Dallas, Texas at a "Love Won Out" conference put on Focus of the Family, a Christian ministry steeped in "traditional Judeo Christian values." Love Won Out was the Boulder, Colorado-based ministry's outreach to people like myself at the time, people struggling to be "delivered" from homosexuality. I couldn't have been more than 23 or 24 at the time. I attended the conference out of desperation as much as curiosity. I participated in one session after another where various alleged formerly gay Christians shared their stories of God's grace and deliverance from the abomination that was homosexuality. They were promoting "conversion therapy," a harmful and ineffective counseling practice that has the nefarious goal of forcing LGBTQ people to deny their personal truth, suppress their homosexuality, and do the impossible: become "straight."

Today, the ex-gay Christianity movement is a shell of its former self. The most notoriously harmful ministries have disbanded or retreated, leaders have abandoned the movement and embraced their queer sexuality anew; and many Christian leaders and organizations are reluctant to be affiliated with the movement's most damaging practices. Ultimately, they fear being branded as homophobic or intolerant. Yet, a simple Internet search will return many horror stories of LGBTQ people who have reported suffering psychological harm as a result of participating in these programs and ministries.

Make no mistake about it: ex-gay therapy is not a relic of the past. It is a destructive practice that is seeking a resurrection in a modern incarnation that eschews the damage of the past and is being rebranded in certain corners of American evangelicalism. Yet what lies just beneath the surface is the same message of self-hate and disenfranchisement from God and a community of faith that has damaged or destroyed many lives over many decades: If you're a Christian with same-sex attractions, change is both possible and necessary.

There are fundamental truths — ugly and harmful ones — that come to light in this reading as the author shares his own dispiriting experiences with the one of the post prominent ex-gay ministries, Exodus International. That is why *Godly...But Gay* is both timely and vital. Many LGBTQ people of faith struggle to reconcile their sexuality with the vociferous, anti-gay doctrines that underpin their religious belief systems.

To be sure, being a gay Christian can be a soul-crushing and deeply agonizing existence. In this book my dear friend and former neighbor, the author of this seminal work and himself a former Independent Baptist pastor, Joel Barrett, sets out in careful and thoughtful detail to help every reader of this book do what he has done: *reclaim his life and his faith*. And in so doing, not only does he give the queer believer the permission they may be waiting for to explore faith, but he also offers a clear and compelling roadmap for those who have found faith to more boldly express it. Indeed, *Godly...But Gay* is an invitation for the queer believer to reevaluate and, if desired, revive their faith.

D. Rashaan Gilmore, Bible School Reject and Proud Christian Homo, Founder and CEO of BlaqOut

TABLE OF CONTENTS

The moment I been waiting on
And my soul is over flowing
With anxieties and expectations
I'm full of desires
I just want it so bad
You know
And it just seems so real
It's right there
I just want reach out and touch it
Before it all disappears

Sometimes It feels like
Everything is passing me by
Every now and then
It feels like
My ship has gone and sailed away

—K'Jon, "On the Ocean"

PRAYER

"Please, kill me, God."

PROLOGUE
The Beginning of the End

"I just want somebody to care about me!"

From the crumpled heap of a man on the basement steps beneath me came the anguishing cry. The words were simple, but the pain was deep. Words melted into sobs of guttural, almost primal noises rising from the darkness deep within.

I barely recognized the man. As I looked down on him, instead of compassion, I felt disgust.
He was weak. He was vulnerable. He was powerless. I hated him. He was everything I was determined not to be.

But he was me.

I heard the words coming from my own mouth but they were foreign to me. In silent incredulity I asked, "Where did *that* come from?! Get ahold of yourself!" I raised my hand to slap the blubbering face in front of me.

The panicked, high-pitched voice of my wife, Dee, at the top of the stairs jerked me back into my own skin.

"What are you talking about?!" She shouted, "I care about you!"

Hands up in exasperation, she stood staring wide-eyed and bewildered at the unrecognizable shadow of the man she married a decade earlier.

It was true, she did care about me. She loved me deeply. She knew me better than anyone else. Yet she did not know me. No one was allowed to know me. I was only beginning to understand how little I knew myself.

Melting on the steps, I sobbed and trembled from the adrenaline rushing through my body. Dee moved to descend the steps in my direction. "Just leave me alone!" I shrieked. She paused, backed away and slowly shut the door behind her.

I stumbled down the remaining steps and curled up into a ball on the sofa in the dark of my basement office. Alone, I moaned and wept until I had no more tears to cry. The pain turned to fear. My mind was flooded with questions I had no answer for.

"What is happening to me?"

"What have I done?"

"Why am I like this?"

I knew there was no turning back now. My worst fears were now a reality. She now knew I had a secret and she was determined to find out what it was. I only wanted to disappear.

"Please, kill me, God." I pleaded.

Death seemed like the only real solution to my problems.

PRAYER

"Lord, I pray for my future wife wherever she may be. Please bring me a tall, beautiful woman who sings soprano and will serve you with me in the church. One who loves you like I do. Lord, protect my future wife wherever she is. Help her stay true to you. Keep her clean and pure for me. Keep her safe. In Jesus' name, Amen."

CHAPTER 1
Do the right thing!

Our perfect marriage began in 1989. She was the first and only girl I dated. My conservative parents did not allow me to date in high school. That wasn't a problem for me because girls were of no interest to me. I was homeschooled and attended tiny churches where there were seldom kids my age to socialize with. I lived in solitude much of the time. The piano and sexual fantasies were my best friends.

I always knew I was gay, although I didn't know that term or use it in association with myself. But from my earliest memories I knew I was different from other boys. It was my shameful secret that no one must ever know. I spent my life trying to distract from my secret. I dressed conservatively, avoiding "feminine" colors. I feigned interest in sports, hunting, and other "manly" activities. I learned to carry my books at my side, not at my chest "like a girl". I tried not to cross my legs "like a woman". I lowered my voice and worked hard to not "sound gay". I painted my office in dark, "masculine" colors. At home, I arranged flowers for the dining room table and told my wife to accept any compliments and not reveal that her husband was responsible for them. I walked with purpose, crossed my arms, stood tall, and spread my legs when I sat all in an attempt to hide my secret.

During my isolated teen years, I convinced myself that my sexual attractions to men were somehow related to my sheltered upbringing and lack of exposure to other Christian young people. I couldn't wait to leave my Effingham, Illinois existence and start afresh in Jacksonville, Florida at Trinity Baptist College where I would be surrounded by godly students who shared my desire to serve the Lord. Their enthusiastic commitment combined with the Biblical teaching and preaching would be a utopian-like environment where I would certainly no longer struggle with the sin of my youth. Instead, I found myself surrounded by a plethora of handsome, young, Bible-toting men in suits and ties--which only awakened my desires even more.

I know what the problem is! I haven't ever dated a girl. Or at least that is what I told myself. Between the preachers in the pulpit and my parents, it was pounded into my head that it was not good for a man to even touch a woman unless she was his wife. I took great pride in never thinking lustful thoughts about women and justified that no one ever told me not to think lustful thoughts about men so I could feel slightly less guilt about that.

Now I just needed to find a girl to date so I could allow myself to be interested and attracted to the opposite sex. That experience would transform me and my desires. I looked forward to asking God to forgive me for lusting after my girlfriend. It would be a welcome change of sin.

I met Dee the week I arrived at Trinity Baptist College. We both received a scholarship to travel around the United States with the Aletheian Singers every weekend of the school year and for up to 8 weeks in the summer. The ensemble's purpose was to represent the college and recruit students from the independent, fundamental, Baptist churches we sang in.

Dee's beautiful smile and height caught my attention the moment I saw her. I quickly did a mental scan of "the checklist". I first began compiling it in my teen years because preachers in the pulpit would say, "God has chosen someone just for you. There is only one person for you. If you marry the wrong person you'll be out of God's will and miserable for the rest of your life." Here is where the preacher would insert a dramatic, anecdotal story of some badly-paired couple who could never be used by God because their lives were ruined because they were never meant to be together. "It's imperative that you pray for your future wife that God will lead you to one another. Pray that she will love God and keep herself clean and pure for you. Pray for her everyday."

I figured if I was going to pray for this person I should let God know the kind of woman I wanted him to bring to me. My daily prayer went something like this: "Lord, I pray for my future wife wherever she may be. Please bring me a tall, beautiful woman who sings soprano and will serve you with me in the church. One who loves you like I do. Lord, protect my future wife wherever she is. Help her stay true to you. Keep her clean and pure for me. Keep her safe. In Jesus' name, Amen."

Dee seemed to check off every box on my list:

✓ Godly? Check. (Not sure how one determines this, but she looked and seemed godly to me.)

✓ Tall? Check. (She was nearly 5'11" and I'm 6'5". We were going to make an impressive looking couple.)

✓ Held to the same Biblical standards and convictions that I did? Check. (This list was many and varied. These were moving targets according to what the latest preacher had determined was important. But she seemed to match more than most did since my list was longer than most.)

✓ Dressed like a modest, godly lady? Check. (This meant she didn't wear pants, only skirts and dresses or culottes for activities. Culottes were somewhat problematic for me because my dad said if you can't do it in a skirt then you shouldn't be doing it. I wasn't quite sure I agreed, so her wearing culottes was not a deal-breaker. She looked and acted feminine in the way that preachers determined women should look and act. She did wear more makeup and jewelry than I thought was necessary and her Princess Diana hairstyle was a little on the too short side, but overall she seemed like the "virtuous woman" described in Proverbs 31. If so, she would likely be submissive to her husband (me), who would be the head of the home as the Bible mandated.)

✓ Sang Soprano? Check. (I sang baritone/tenor and I needed a soprano who could duet with me. She had a beautiful, strong soprano voice that brought chills to my spine. Oh - and bonus points for her impressive piano skills. This would certainly make us a power-couple in ministry.)

✓ Pretty? Check. (While I was never sexually attracted to a female, I did appreciate her feminine beauty. She always made a great first impression, had a great smile, and knew how to present herself well. I knew she and I would look good together.)

Everyone at the small college immediately paired us and pushed us to one another. They thought we made the ideal couple - mostly because we were both tall. They knew little else about me.

We began spending time together and quickly discovered that we shared many common interests and likes in music, style, decor, and fashion so we enjoyed our time together around those things. Our friendship quickly developed into a courtship. We were dating. Everyone was excited to see us paired.

By the end of my Freshman year it was hard for me to imagine that there could be a better fit for me, so surely, she must be the one God had been saving for me. She must be the answer to my prayers, if only I *wanted* to be with a woman. While I enjoyed our romantic friendship, when I lie in bed at night masturbating, my fantasies were filled with the images of the naked men who shared the dorm showers with me every morning.

I won't be like this once I can actually have sex with a woman. I'm only this way because I've kept myself so pure and never allowed myself to think about having sex with a woman because that would be lustful. I rationalized. I set my sights on marrying Dee. It was the only logical choice and solution to my problem. And I think I do really love her.

As was typical with most independent Baptist colleges, off campus dates were discouraged but were allowed after requesting permission, obtaining an approved chaperone, identifying where the date would take place, and how long the three of you would be off campus. No physical contact was allowed between members of the opposite sex at any time. Only during meals and designated hours were members of the opposite sex allowed to socialize in the common areas of the main building. Dorms were strictly off limits to non-residents.

Every effort was made to insure that no touching, hand holding, kissing, and certainly no pre-marital sex took place. However, this didn't stop it from happening completely. Nearly every semester someone would be written up or even kicked out of school for the violation of one or more of these rules. I had no trouble abiding by the rules since I never desired to break them, but some of my dorm mates found it much more difficult to resist the temptation. They found secret places to steal a quick hug and kiss with their girlfriends and of course, the bragging commenced.

"So Joel, have you and Dee kissed yet?"

I felt my face grow flush. "No! We want to wait until our wedding day! But I sure wish I could. It's so hard to resist." Hoping I sounded convincing enough.

"Oh come on Joel, how are you going to wait for that? Don't you want to kiss her now? You have a long way to wait until you get married! Besides, how do you know if you want to buy the car if you haven't taken her for a test drive?"

At that moment I realized the truth; I needed to kiss her whether I wanted to or not. She was a good companion and friend and I loved her, but the thought of kissing her did nothing for me. Then the horrible realization came that if I didn't express the same barely controlled passions and desire that these guys did, maybe they would suspect I was gay. That kiss would prove to me, her, and my friends that I was not gay.

"I will probably kiss her soon. I really want to so much, but I'm trying to respect our commitment to wait until marriage. We want our first kiss to be at the wedding altar. But I may not be able to wait." I played this conversation over and over again in my mind wondering if my friends really believed me. What if they suspected I was gay? I was determined to find an opportunity to kiss Dee so I could go back and report it to my friends as proof that I was just as straight as any of them. I was also hoping that a kiss would awaken some unknown attractions and I'd no longer scroll through my memory bank of all the images of naked, lean, muscular, men I had collected over the years.

One night, a couple of weeks later, we found a creative way to have a date without a chaperone. On a bridge by a stream, we kissed. Much to my dismay, instead of sparks and passion I felt guilt. I had broken the college rules, gone against my principles, and ruined our chances of bragging at our wedding that we had never kissed until that day. She seemed to feel all the right things yet I felt nothing, but I was happy to go back to the guys and share my exaggerated report that my passions had gotten the best of me and that I had finally made out with my girlfriend.

"It was amazing. We kissed and hugged in the moonlight. No one saw us. She wanted more, I mean we both wanted more, but I dared not go any further or I'd never be able to stop. Man, it was good. I can't wait to get married!" They seemed adequately impressed and offered a roar of hearty congratulations on my achievement. I was relieved. If they believed I was straight, maybe I could change myself to be who they thought I was.

I returned to my dorm room and masturbated to the image of the tall, olive-skinned, well-endowed, Italian basketball player I often saw in the shower because I timed my morning shower time to match his. I convinced myself that the guilt and lack of passion from kissing my girlfriend was the Holy Spirit convicting me of not "saving myself" for marriage. Not to mention breaking the college rules.

The rest of my time in college was spent being a thoughtful boyfriend who sent cards and letters to his girlfriend and doted over her in every way possible, all the while thinking about the masculine, soapy bodies I saw in the dorm shower, the images from the gay porn magazine I opened at the magazine stand, or the men who gave me a show at the urinal in the mall restroom.

In 1989 we said, "I do" at a large independent, fundamental, Baptist church in Macon, Georgia where my future wife taught fifth grade in a Christian school. The night before our wedding I stayed at my best friend's home and pondered how good it would feel to finally have sex with the woman I loved and be rid of these gay desires once and for all. I was convinced it would magically go away after our wedding night. I decided I might as well enjoy my last night as a single man. My hand and some R-rated movie on cable TV that showed more skin than usual were the perfect way to get off one last time before my overnight transformation.

It was a Saturday evening and a candlelight ceremony that was far more elaborate than I wanted, but Dee was determined to fulfill all of her romantic ideals of the perfect wedding and I went along with it. I truly wanted her to be happy. The wedding was a sea of pink and white flowers, teal taffeta gowns, black tailed tuxedos and glowing candles. The ceremony included several songs, a harpist, and two officiants. The six groomsmen included my best friends from college. Years later three of the men involved in my wedding party and numerous college friends who attended the wedding also came out as gay or lesbian. I guess LGBT birds of a feather really do flock together.

I stood with the groomsmen and my dad in a side room off the platform waiting for the designated moment we were to walk out on stage and take our place. "Dad, any last minute advice for me?" I asked as he straightened my bow-tie. My Dad was a stern but loving man of few words and prone to angry outbursts. I could tell the question caught him off guard. He paused, chuckled a bit and replied, "Just remember son: sometimes it's just best to just admit you're wrong - even if you aren't - to keep peace." Although peaceful is not how I would describe my parents' relationship, it seemed like good advice to me at the time because I vividly remembered him doing this (albeit grudgingly) many times over the years.

The wedding coordinator interrupted our moment and we walked out in single file to take our place on the stage. My insides quivered with a ball of emotions that ranged from excitement and anticipation to fear and shame. *I'm doing the right thing, right? Everything will be different after tonight, right?* But it was too late to think about that now. The bridesmaids had taken their place. The familiar *dum-da-dum-dum-dum* of the wedding march began and was immediately accompanied by the whooshing sound of 200 people standing to their feet, looking to the back of the sanctuary where Dee was making her way down the aisle in a white, lacy gown entirely hand-sewn by her mother. I smiled nervously as my insides shook. This was the moment I had waited for.

We exchanged traditional vows and sealed it in a simple kiss that felt to me more awkward than romantic. The minister who was Dee's childhood youth pastor pronounced us husband and wife to the joyful applause of the audience. By the time we arrived at the wedding suite in the stately Victorian home converted into an inn, we were both exhausted but happy. We did love one another. I was certain that from now on, I would be the best husband in the world and make her the happiest wife in the world. I determined that this would be my focus and everything else would fall into place. I spent my abstinent youth convincing myself that once I was with a woman my desires for men would magically disappear. To my dismay, they did not.

I poured my heart and soul into my marriage, finishing college, and accepting the new position of Assistant Pastor at a large church in Peoria, Illinois that waited for me immediately following graduation. The newness of everything distracted me for a month or two. I felt good that my masturbation habit had decreased because of these new beginnings, but it bothered me that I still found myself noticing every handsome man in any environment; stealing an occasional peak at a Playgirl magazine at Walden Books; stopping by cruisy bathrooms hoping to catch a glimpse of other interested men and following it all up with a tearful prayer to God, begging forgiveness and promising to never let it happen again. I was even more disheartened that months after my wedding I was still struggling with my desires for men. *It's just the stress of finishing school, but when I get in ministry, that will stop it.* This was the new lie I told myself. *I'll be so consumed with the responsibility of leading others and making a home with my wife that there will be no way I could think these thoughts. I have an important job to do. That will change everything.* And so I looked forward to our move from Florida to Illinois and all the positive change it would bring.

We arrived in Peoria and began our life in ministry together. I led the music, directed the choir, developed a young adult ministry, coordinated a

Wednesday night kids program, visited the sick and elderly, occasionally filled the pulpit, and anything else that fell under the broad umbrella of pastoral duties. My wife played the piano, sang, and assisted me in most of my ministry efforts.

By all outward appearances, my wife and I had the ideal ministry marriage. I was determined to be everything a good, godly husband should be. I provided for her. I read the Christian marriage books and worked on communication and understanding her. I supported her interests. I praised her publicly. I showed her affection. I bought her gifts. I had sex with her.

We did everything together. We sang together. We accompanied one another on the piano. We ministered together. We looked good together. We even taught other couples how to have a successful marriage. It was obvious to all that we were meant to be together for the glory of God. We were respected and revered in our fundamentalist circles.

To my dismay, being married and in ministry didn't wash away my desires altogether. The guilt and shame returned full force right along with my wife's announcement that we were going to have a baby! The thought of being a dad both excited and scared me. *I'm going to be responsible for a little human being!* With that realization came the new lie I told myself: *Being a dad is such a huge responsibility. I'm going to have to be the best example ever to my child. This is going to change everything.* I believed this lie too. After the birth of our third child I knew that no matter how many children we had, I would still be who I was and carry my secret. Fatherhood had not changed this part of me.

I found solace in cruising parks and restrooms for quick, anonymous, sexual, encounters with other men seeking the same. When humans are denied the right to be who they are, it doesn't stop their desires and needs. It just pushes them to find creative ways to have those needs met. Gays cruising for sex in parks and public restrooms, while extremely risky, was the only way gay men - especially closeted gay men - could have their needs met. If this is news to you, no fear - I'll unpack the history and more in the pages to come.

The risk of being caught having sex in a public place was great, but the reward was greater. I had countless sexual encounters during my closeted life. They were exhilarating and satisfying in the moment, but within moments of zipping up my pants the euphoria gave way to extreme guilt, shame, and fear. Guilt for not being a good, godly man. Shame for who I was. Fear of being discovered and losing everything.

After nearly a decade of ministry in central Illinois we moved to Northern Indiana to "plant" a brand-new church. I was excited for this move because it felt like a clean slate, a fresh start for me. *Joel, this is the chance you've been waiting for. You are going to a new place where you don't know anyone and no one knows you. You don't know the cruising spots. You have a completely clean slate and a fresh start. This will be your life's work and your last chance, now don't mess it up!*

Planting a church was an enormous project that stretched my wife and I beyond our limits. In just under three years we gathered a growing congregation, established by-laws, obtained a building and property, held multiple, weekly services, and became a self-supporting church. We poured our heart, soul, and entire bank account into the endeavor.

Dee homeschooled our three children and was responsible for the music, children's, and ladies' ministries in our small, growing church. In addition to being a husband and father, my days were consumed with preparing sermons and leadership materials, counseling the congregation, directing the praise team, leading the organizational structure of the church, and outreach in the community.

Life was full of responsibility. We were a respected couple in the ministry world. Other pastors were certain that we'd build a large, thriving, church and minister well into our old age. We were the good, godly pastor's family that everyone admired - or so it appeared. Externally, I was doing everything right. Internally, I was crumbling. With each new stress of building a church, ministering to the congregation, and maintaining a family--my desire to find relief grew even stronger. My lifelong companions - sexual fantasy and masturbation -

were happy to step in and provide that temporary escape to my increasingly miserable reality of self-sacrifice. I was growing progressively disenchanted with ministry as an occupation. Planting and growing a church was grueling and relentless. Starting a new church is very much like starting a new business. It takes a team of people, lots of money, effective marketing, customer service, resulting in a higher level of expectation every time the doors are open. Dee was spread too thin as well. Not only was she homeschooling our three children, but also deeply involved in the daily operations of the ministry. We made a dynamic ministry team. For us, each service or meeting was a themed event. We were creative extroverts, so performing was in our blood. We enjoyed the process and the final product, but ministry often feels like being "on" 24/7 - which no one can do for long. The pressure of living in a fish bowl and constantly being "on" added another layer of stress on our dying relationship, which only produced more conflict and drove us further apart. Our friendship, which was the glue of our marriage, became suffocating to me. Everything felt like work.

I slowly fell back into my old ways. I found the parks and restrooms where sexual encounters were likely to occur. I found reasons to drive by or stop at these places as often as I could. It was around 2000 when dial up internet became a household necessity. I descended to my office in the basement of our home which was merely a small area of a large open room designated to be used as my office. It was a "finished" basement only because it had 1950s checkerboard tile flooring, blond wood paneling, and a drop ceiling with those interlocking tile squares that looked somewhat padded. In the corner near the area I used as my office there was a large, unused fireplace. The only outside light came from two tiny, ground-level windows on the north side of the home. My desk and the coordinating credenza were strategically placed to shield my computer from view should my wife or children come downstairs. I spent hours each day sitting there in the solitude, studying my Bible and preparing sermons with help from the new online sermon prep sites to better interpret the scriptures, find pithy illustrations, search sermon topics, read Bible commentaries, and even download someone else's sermon to edit and make my own. This new online world also gave me instant easy access to free gay websites, porn, chat rooms and very thorough directories of where to cruise for sex anywhere in the world.

The screeching and beeping of the dial up modem became the alluring sound of my escape from my stressful, ministry reality into a strange world of gay men all over the world (and locally) who didn't know me as dad, husband, or pastor Joel. Instead, they knew me as Tall Ben 66. Tall Ben was in his 30s, 6'5" tall, 210lbs, hairy, fit, and full of flirtatious charm. In the chat room, I was desired. I was fresh meat. Men were infatuated by height. I took quickly to the rhythm of a chat room which was a welcome distraction from the Bible and study books off to the side. Like a dance, I moved from the Word document containing the beginnings of Sunday's sermon to the portal for the world wide web. I made sure I had multiple bible related tabs open convincing myself that I would study while I chatted with men in the Gay.com chat window. *I'm good at multitasking and besides there's nothing wrong with talking to people, after all, that's all I'm doing.*

Within minutes of settling in, the dings of the chatroom notifications lured me away from my Bible and into numerous, sexy chat conversations with men near me. They loved me. I was new and different. They wanted me. I carefully navigated around any questions that would give away too much of my identity. It was like a window into a world I had been denied all of my life. Minutes turned into hours. I felt guilty that I wasn't working on my sermon. *I know what I'm going to say, I just need to finish writing it down. I can do that in a few minutes, I'll wrap up this conversation soon.*

The footsteps on the kitchen floor above me was my alert to my wife approaching the basement door at the top of the stairs. Without any warning to the men I was in mid-chat with, I exited all the windows except the Bible study ones and put my Bible on my lap. The footsteps above me walked back across the floor. *False alarm! Great, now I need to go back to gay.com and let those guys know that I didn't mean to suddenly disappear so they won't think I'm an asshole.*

It was nearly a fail-proof system IF I always erase my browser history AND clear cookies when I stepped away because I was not the only one using the computer. More than once I had a moment of panic when my wife went to use the computer and I couldn't remember if I had erased my digital footprints from earlier in the day.

The world of chat rooms gave me the opportunity to hide behind my computer, assume an anonymous profile name, and chat in real time with other gay men. While it didn't completely stop my cruising, it brought much of it to me instead of me having to go find it. The intervals between points of desperation were growing shorter. Sex had become my drug. My escape. My life was now a string of hookups. I planned my week, even my day, around them. If I could have hooked up more than once in a day I would have. And sometimes I did. I wasted hours on gay.com chatting with strangers, making virtual friends and cruising for my next hookup. It was the only "safe" way of finding relief. Every encounter, I swore to God, was my last.

PRAYER

"Please forgive me God. It won't happen again."

CHAPTER 2
The Hookup

As the dial-up modem screeched and beeped, I sat in excited anticipation of what handsome flesh might be awaiting me in my virtual gay bar. Once inside Gay.com, I quickly scanned the creative screen names of the local men ready hanging out in the chat room.

Hung4Hung.

Twinkboi.

SirCumsalot.

MascTop2000.

I was TallBen66, a reference to my height, my middle name, and the year of my birth.

Ignoring the photo-less profiles like my own, I hurriedly clicked on the others, revealing their enlarged photo. I mentally ranked each as hot, kind of hot, or not hot.

No, not him. Eww, he's old and fat.

Hmm, he's really hot! Probably too hot for me though.

Oh he's really cute, but I'm sure I'm too old for him.

Oh! Who's this? I don't recall seeing him here before.

Not bad, I'll come back to him after I explore the others.

Each click was followed by a quick review of the stats listed on their profile. Age? I preferred someone my age or hopefully younger...of course. Height? Weight? These two mattered because - when factored together - it told me if the guy was properly proportioned. That was very important to me because I certainly didn't want anyone "fat".

Physical description? This was difficult to decode without seeing more photos, but I quickly learned that swimmer's build was code for skinny. Football build was code for fat. Muscular was code for anything from going to the gym on occasion or being a gym rat.

Sexual preferences? This category could include as little or as much as the user wanted to share. Most guys listed top, bottom, or versatile here. They also might include things like an interest in kink, leather, bondage, or drugs. Other details included community sub-group identifiers like: bear, twink, otter, daddy, sub, and a host of other strange labels that often required me to do a quick internet search. Some put it all out there, others held their cards close.

Once I determined who was fuckable, the private messages began:

Hey.

Hi.

What's up?

Nothing much. Just bored LOL.

Yeah. Me too. LOL. Great pic! Looking good.

Thanks, you too. Any more pics? (This of course, meant nude pics)

Pics were exchanged with exclamations of "hot!", "mmm", or "Nice cock!"

The chat quickly devolved into mostly sexually charged banter and innuendo that ultimately lead to talk of specific sexual preferences like, "Top or bottom?" "What are you into?" The big question was "What are you looking for?" which determined if hooking up was the next step or not.

On this particular occasion, the rendezvous was arranged at a half-way point between our homes. I made up an excuse to run an errand which took me to a K-Mart parking lot 10 miles from my home and church. It wasn't the most desirable arrangement, but I was desperate. Again.

The sun reflected off the bleached pavement with rows of faded yellow markings. The handful of cars and Wednesday afternoon shoppers made it easy to spot the blue conversion van described earlier to me in the chat room. For me, it was just another hookup. Not unlike the many, many before it: Quick. Discreet. Anonymous.

Pulling up beside his van, we nodded in recognition, relieved that each resembled our profile photos. As I climbed into the passenger seat, my heart skipped, a chill traveled down my spine and a knot formed in my stomach. I couldn't explain it, but I sensed I was looking at myself in the mirror.

He is you. The voice inside my head startled me. I looked at this complete stranger (who I later learned was named Kevin) and couldn't shake the feeling that we were the same person. The uneasy look in his eyes told me he felt the same.

There is an unwritten code of conduct for cruising hookups. No one speaks of it, but everyone agrees to it. The code is: We meet. We get off. We exchange no personal information. We avoid most small talk. And most importantly: if we ever see one another anywhere else in public, we pretend we've never met and that this hookup never happened.

But we were here to get it on ... so ignoring the knot in my stomach, we pulled around to the back of K-Mart and climbed into the back seats of the van. We groped and kissed in a fit of wild passion, fingers fumbling with buttons, zippers and belts until there was nothing between us. Skin on skin, our bodies entwined, we explored every inch of one another, touching, tasting, breathing in the scent of our hot, sweaty, male bodies. The windows of the rocking van grew steamy as we released our passions in grunts and groans of pure ecstasy. It was the kind of good, glorious sex that can only be had when there is great risk involved. It was over quicker than either of us desired, but it was good. It was really good. As we wiped the sweat from our faces and searched for our scattered clothing, we engaged in a bit of mundane, small talk while attempting to reassemble ourselves into the respectable men we purported to be. We both sensed there was common ground between us despite not having revealed any significant personal information. I weighed the consequences, took the risk, and broke the code.

The exchange began like a ping pong game in slow motion:

"I'm married."

"So am I."

"I have three young children."

"I have two."

"I've been this way my whole life and I'm so scared of anyone finding out because it would cost me everything."

"Me too."

He turned in his seat, looked dead in my face and said,

"I'll tell you what I do if you tell me first."

Swallowing the lump in my throat I replied, "I'm in Communications...but not in the way you think. I'm...a Baptist minister."

His eyes widened. "I am a Methodist minister."

He was me. I was him.

In stunned silence, we breathed in the awful truth while still heavy with the scent of our sexual climax just moments before.

Despite the shock, a strange sense of relief flooded over me. Never had I been that honest and transparent with anyone. For the first time in my life, someone knew and understood me. I wasn't alone anymore. This was both comforting and frightening. I felt naked and vulnerable as if suddenly the whole world knew I was gay.

"What do we do now?" I asked.

"We can't go on like this," he replied.

"We need help or we're going to lose everything." He nodded in agreement. We both knew that this was not who we wanted to be. We were fully aware that our marriages, families, careers, and reputations were precariously at risk. In an "I will if you will" kind of way we agreed to support one another in our efforts to get help. I wasn't sure what help would look like or if it was even possible, but I knew I had to give it one last try.

I drove home cold and quivering from the adrenaline rushing through my body. I knew I must act immediately before I talked myself out of taking action. While in my office, I did what I did what any godly minister would do: I called Exodus International, the world's largest ex-gay ministry. I knew it was my only option and my final attempt at fixing myself. Hands trembling, I held the phone, counting the rings and hoping no one would answer. A recorded message on an answering machine confirmed the right number had been dialed.

Hang up! screamed the voice inside me. The machine beeped. Pushing my lips close to the receiver, I cupped my hands around my mouth to avoid being heard. In a hushed voice I said, "My name is Joel. I'd like to talk with someone about my...struggles. I'm not sure how to do this. I'm married and my wife doesn't know about my struggles so please call me back at this number and let me know when I can talk to someone." I hurriedly left my office phone number and a good time to call me and hung up. In a state of panic, more adrenaline rushed through my veins. My entire body shook and quivered uncontrollably. I felt cold and hot all at once.

What did I just do?! I asked myself. I fought the desire to call back and say, "Please ignore my previous message and do not call me back." My mind raced around like a pinball bouncing from pin to pin. *Maybe they won't get the voicemail. Maybe they'll accidentally delete the voicemail and not be able to call me back. You tried. If they don't call back, you can say you tried, just don't ever do that again!*

I hoped beyond hope that I would never receive a return phone call and could put this moment behind me. I believed I would somehow be relieved of responsibility because I had reached out and no one had responded. I would go back to my secret ways and hide even deeper in the closet. No one had to know about me. I composed myself and went back to my daily routine, but despite my best efforts of ignoring it, something in me had changed. Deep inside, a scared little boy named Joel was huddled in the corner shaking and crying in fear of the unknown. He knew he was about to be exposed and it scared him to death.

A few days later, my hopes of being lost in the shuffle were dashed when, as I listened to my voicemails, I heard the calm and pleasant voice of the Indiana state director for Exodus International return my call with instructions on when I should call him back. I was surprised and yet relieved that his voice was more youthful and "gay sounding" than I expected. I sensed he would understand my situation. I was correct. He did.

There's things that you guess
And things that you know
There's boys you can trust
And girls that you don't
There's little things you hide
And little things that you show
Sometimes you think you're gonna get it
But you don't and that's just the way it goes
I want your sex.
        — George Michael, I Want Your Sex

PRAYER

Prayer to self: 'This is your last chance, Joel, don't f*ck it up.'

The best way out is always through.
— Robert Frost

CHAPTER 3
First Experiences with Exodus International

It was Focus on the Family that first introduced me to Exodus International. The internet made it easier to quietly follow their ministry and others like it for a number of years. I hoped I might learn the secret to overcoming my homosexuality without having to bring anyone else into my reality.

In our first conversation and email exchange, Brad invited me to attend a conference he was coordinating for ministry leaders. The title and description implied that it was designed to help pastors and church leaders like learn about current culture and how to better minister. Later, I realized the real purpose of the conference was to provide a safe space for ministers like me to get help for their struggles without drawing attention to themselves. I was thankful for that. I got up early that morning and drove the three hours from South Bend to Indianapolis. My stomach quivered in a ball of nerves. I felt bad for keeping my wife in the dark about the true nature of my trip. She knew I was seeing a counselor who had invited me to attend a "pastoral conference on culture and sexuality" but what she didn't know was that the counselor was the state leader for Exodus International, the largest ex-gay ministry/network in the world at that time. The Exodus Conference featured the popular speaker Sy Rogers and a series of workshops.

Brad said we could meet the following day for a counseling session.

Turning off the car, I sat frozen in the seat staring at the strange but typical 1980s style architecture of the church building with its high-pitched roof creating an impractical triangular entrance. I intentionally arrived just minutes before the conference start-time. The last thing I wanted to do was be forced to have casual conversation with anyone. *What if someone in there recognizes me? How will I explain why I am there?* I waited until another late-comer began walking toward the entrance to hop out of my car, keeping just the right amount of distance between me and them to avoid conversation. I paused at the door, tried to calm my nerves, took a deep breath and walked in. Before I could turn back I was greeted by a very enthusiastic--and very effeminate--man. He was one of the gayest men I had met at that point in my life. Next to him was a manly woman with shorter hair.

"Hello! Welcome! Let's get you registered." He said as he pushed a program at me and asked for my name and email.

"Brad Grammer invited me to this. Is he around?" I asked, trying to sound as casual and nonchalant as possible despite my nerves.

"Brad? Yes, actually that's him right over there." He gestured across the foyer to a young, attractive man engaged in conversation with someone else. I finished the paperwork, grabbed the program guide and asked where I should go.

"Right through those doors over there by Brad. You're going to love Sy, he's an amazing speaker. You're going to have a great day, now hurry on in, they're just about ready to start." I walked to Brad and introduced myself.

"Joel! It's great to see you. We'll catch up after this session, why don't you head on in now?" I entered the auditorium and quickly took a seat near the back hoping no one would notice me. Out of caution, I scanned the audience for familiar faces as I was accustomed to doing in any new environment. I wasn't looking for friends; I was nervously searching for any faces that might know my secret. I lived in constant fear of being outed by someone who knew me from gay.com, a cruisy spot, or a hookup. To my relief, it was a room full of strangers. The energy in the room felt awkward and stressful.

Brad walked to the platform and welcomed the crowd. *He sounds a little gay, but he's kind of cute.* I thought to myself. *What are you doing Joel?! You can't be lusting after your counselor. You ought to be ashamed of yourself. You can't even get help without thinking lustful thoughts. You are so disgusting.* I promptly refocused and asked God to forgive me for thinking such a lustful thought. I was determined to keep my eyes off the men around me and focus on the purpose of the meeting. Before I could think any more self-deprecating thoughts, a short introductory video began playing on the large screen hanging above the choir loft. The video told the dramatic and colorful story of Sy Rogers, a very feminine man who lived a life torn between presenting as a man or as a woman. I sat stunned as photos of him living as a beautiful woman filled the screen. The somber music changed to an upbeat, hopeful tune as we were informed that he found Jesus just days away from having reassignment surgery to become a woman. I sat pondering the video trying to hide my shock and discomfort. My deep thought was broken by the high-pitched, shockingly feminine voice of Sy as he took the microphone. I sat back stunned. *What is this? THIS is a man who is telling me how not to be gay anymore? He's the most feminine, gay-sounding man I've ever heard!*

I was disappointed. This was not what I wanted. So far everyone I encountered at this conference was gayer than the gay men I hooked up with on gay.com. But I knew this was my last chance to get help, so I committed to giving it my full attention despite my disappointment and skepticism.

I don't remember much of what Sy said, but I was taken aback by his honesty and transparency. He spared nothing from his story. I had never heard anyone speak so openly about sexuality and their personal sexual history, especially in the pulpit of a church. I began letting down my guard as I listened. The more I listened the less I noticed his feminine mannerisms and speaking style. I didn't relate to his story, but I thought if God could make him straight then surely he could make anyone straight. But I secretly hoped I would become A LOT more convincingly straight than the men at the conference.

After he spoke I stayed behind to talk with him. He took my hand and listened while intently looking deep into my eyes as if he were seeing into my soul. To my surprise I felt no judgement, only compassion. This was foreign to me, but it was the magic key that unlocked my emotions and my tongue. As tears streamed down my face I poured what I felt were the relevant highlights of my life to him: *I don't know what to do, I've been this way for as long as I can remember. I grew up in a very conservative, Baptist home and never felt like I could talk to anyone about this sin. I've tried everything. I don't want to be like this. I hate who I am, but I don't know what to do. If anyone finds out about me, I'm going to lose everything.*

I burst into ugly sobs. As Sy put his hand on my shoulder, he said "It's okay Joel. I understand. You're hurting, aren't you?"

I looked at him through my tears, nodded yes, and collapsed on the front pew crying like I had never cried before. The flood gates had opened and the dam of unacknowledged pain burst out. It wouldn't subside for several years. But for now, I let it flow unashamedly because no one had ever acknowledged my pain before. I had never acknowledged my pain. I focused on the guilt and shame, but never gave myself permission to feel the pain. I didn't deserve to be in pain. It was my sin and I had no right to feel sorry for myself.

As the hot tears flowed down my face, I painted a verbal picture for him of my life up to that point. My judgmental parents who were only happy when they were miserable. My isolated homeschool experience. The hellfire and damnation churches where I grew up that believed someone like me had no place in the Kingdom of God. My sexual exploits which became my only escape but only added shame and fear of being caught.

Sy mostly just listened and said little, but I knew, for the first time in my life, someone was seeing the real me and wasn't rejecting me. He tenderly put his hand on my cheek and said "Joel, God loves you and I love you. You're going to be okay. You're not alone. You're hurting and feeling pain, but that's okay. It's okay to feel that pain. You're in the right place." He assured me that Brad would be able to help me. Before he walked away, he prayed over me and left me there to compose myself. I don't remember anything else from that day.

I left my hotel early the next morning to get to the counselor's office in plenty of time. I sat in the empty parking lot of the warehouse-looking building and waited for Brad to arrive. I knew I was about to embark on an unknown journey that would either fix me once and for all or destroy everything I ever knew and loved.

Don't hold back Joel. This is your last chance. There is no option after this. Tell him everything.

I watched as Brad parked his car, unlocked the building and disappeared inside. I took a deep breath, composed myself, exited my car and made my way inside. Brad was a friendly, compassionate man who spoke of his own youthful struggle with same-sex attraction or SSA as they referred to it. He explained that he was now happily married to his wife and had twin boys. This encouraged me. If Brad could be fixed then maybe I could be too!

"So...what did you think of the conference yesterday?"

"It was interesting.   It gave me a lot to think about."

"How was your conversation with Sy?"
That was all it took for the tears to begin flowing again. *No one has ever made me feel like that before. I've never had anyone show such compassion. For the first time in my life I feel there's hope.* For the next hour I told Brad everything I thought might shed light on why I was the way I was, hoping he might interrupt me at some point and say "That's it! That's why you're gay!"

But he didn't.   Instead, I shared and cried and sobbed. With each story, I became more emotional. It was like an out of body experience. *Who is this man? Why am I crying? What am I saying? No one is supposed to know all this about me.*

"I'm sorry Brad, I don't know why I'm crying."

He was kind, compassionate, and offered no judgement.

"It's pain, Joel. You're in pain."

Pain? I thought. Why should I be in pain? I had no right to feel pain. Others had certainly had far worse lives than me. This was very different from what I had expected. I now realize he had probably heard many stories similar to mine. I was sure that no one had stooped as low as me. I'm sure he was far from shocked as I spilled my guts. That relieved me.

Instead, he sat and listened while occasionally leaning forward and asking "How do you feel about that Joel?" in that stereotypical manner of a therapist.

"I don't know. How should I feel about that?"

"Joel, there is no should. How do you feel about it?"

"I don't know. Should I be angry? Should I be sad?"

"Joel, there is no should, your feelings are not right or wrong, they just are. Now think about it for a moment and then leave the "should" out and just tell me what you feel."

I sat in silence, feeling nothing but confusion.

"I don't know. I don't know what to feel."

It was true. I was dead inside. I had never been allowed to feel. I was told how to feel. I wasn't accustomed to anyone asking how I felt. I had never allowed myself to feel. Feelings, I had been taught, were not to be trusted.

Anger was sinful.

Sadness was discontentment with God.

Happiness was self-serving and fleeting at best.

Fear was distrust of God.

Resentment was a lack of forgiveness.

Confusion was the lack of seeking and knowing God.

Anxiety was the result of not accepting the peace of
God.

There were only three feelings that were allowed. The first was guilt, which was felt when the Holy Spirit convicts you of your sin. The second was joy, which could only happen when you sacrificed your own desires by putting Jesus first, others second and yourself last. And then there was was shame, which you felt for being the horrible, broken sinner that you are. These were the only feelings I knew. The rest were foreign to me. Brad handed me a piece of paper with a list of feelings words on it.

"I want you to use this list to help you identify your feelings. As you go throughout your day and think about things from your past, I want you to stop and look over this list and attempt to attach one or more of these words to your feelings. It's okay to be angry, sad, or anything else you feel." He explained that emotions were from God and that we were allowed to feel them.

He handed me the book "Desires In Conflict" by Joe Dallas, a prominent ex-gay leader at that time. "I want you to read this book and highlight the things that stand out to you. It will help you have a better understanding of yourself and your struggles." I became very familiar with the word *struggle*. The ex-gay movement referred to us as strugglers. I met many fellow strugglers. We all struggled with SSA - Same Sex Attraction. I thumbed through the book, wondering how I was going to hide this book from my wife. She would wonder why I was reading a book about homosexual desires. *My wife! Wait! What am I going to tell her about this weekend?! What am I going to tell her about anything?!*

"I'm not going to have to tell my wife or my church am I?" I blurted out in a total panic.

"I don't know." He replied. "Some do, some don't."

"I can't tell her! I'll lose everything if I tell her." He assured me that there was no need to make that decision at that early stage. The thought of telling anyone but him terrified me.

"Can I be fixed?" I asked.

"Joel, everyone experiences something different. Some go on to lead happy heterosexual lives. Others still struggle with their SSA but have learned to live with it and not act out on it by changing their behaviors and thought patterns. I can't tell you where you will end up, but I can assure you that God did not make you this way and He can help you be who he wants you to be."

The hour in his office felt like ten minutes. It passed so quickly. We exchanged emails and scheduled another appointment in two weeks. Closing the door to his office quietly behind me, I descended the dark steps to the street level, squinting my swollen, tear-washed eyes as I stepped into the full sunlight reflecting off the pavement of the nearly empty parking lot. I pushed my hands deep into my pockets to protect them from the cold Indianapolis air and hurried to my car with weak knees. I started the car and began the three-hour trip home feeling completely drained, exhausted and overwhelmed by it all. In a silent daze, my mind swirled. I thought about Sy Rogers' hand on my cheek. I thought about Brad's list of "feelings words". I thought about all the men I met that seemed so gay to me yet they claimed to be free of their same sex attraction. I thought about Brad. Was that who I was destined to be? Is that even what I wanted?

PRAYER

"God, I'm scum. I hate myself and my sin. I don't want to be this way. Please, forgive me."

There are no unnatural acts, only unacceptable acts.
— Robert Black

CHAPTER 4
The Art of Cruising

I was ten years old when my subtle sexual awakening began. It was a hot, summer day in St. Louis. My best friend John and I grabbed our fishing poles and tackle box, hopped on our bikes and rode to a small local park with a large fishing pond. We had every intention of catching the "big one" that day. Neither of us had any strategy or knowledge of what to do with it if we actually caught it but we were determined to give it an impatient try. It was the thrill of the hunt more than the reward of the catch that drew us there. You never knew what was lurking just beneath the surface of that murky water. Later I learned that fishing was very similar to cruising for sex in that regard.

Nature called, so leaving my rod and reel with my friend I ran around the edge of the pond to the small, concrete building with doors propped open that contained the typical, dirty, smelly toilet and urinal for public use. I stood at the toilet behind the doorless concrete stall and relieved myself. The small vented window nearby cast filtered light on the wall beside me. As my eyes adjusted to the darkness I noticed the walls were covered with words and drawings from previous users who had left their mark there. I'm sure it wasn't the first time I had been to a bathroom with graffiti on the wall, but it was the first time it caught my attention. I stood there, penis still in hand, and let my eyes wonder all over the words and pictures taking them all in. I quickly recognized the theme and variations on a penis. Some drawings were crude and almost unrecognizable while others were detailed works of art.

I was intrigued so I began reading. There were a lot of words that were new, meaningless, yet a little stimulating to me because I instinctively knew they were naughty. In the middle of the sea of ink, was a particularly long and detailed paragraph in fresh, unfaded ink. This made it standout from the other writing on the wall and drew me in. To my surprise, the author of the post extended an open invitation to all readers for a party in his home on an upcoming date at the address listed.

The detailed instructions, as I remember them, explained that no underwear was allowed because attendees were expected to take off their clothes when they arrived. Having only recently discovered the penis between my legs, I was surprised by the growing stiffness I felt in my hand as I read and reread the writing on the wall. I didn't know exactly what it all meant, but I knew my penis and I wanted to know more.

The address was meaningless to me, but I imagined it to be close by. I memorized it. I fantasized about riding my bike to the house the night of the party and hiding in the bushes near the front window. I wouldn't dare go in, but perhaps I could sneak a peek into what I envisioned being a room full of naked boys my age and slightly older frolicking, and playing together. I didn't envision sex because I didn't even know what sex was at that point in my life. But I knew the thought of naked boys did something inside of me.

In the days and weeks after that day of fishing in the park, my mind often wandered to that bathroom wall. Several times I rode my bike back to that park to read it again. Each time it excited me just like the first time.

I began reading bathroom walls everywhere I went. The walls were talking and I was listening. This was the beginning of my sex education. I wasn't sure what it all meant, but I felt a kinship with the unknown author of those crude scribblings. It was the first realization that I was not alone. There were others out there like me. There were men who liked men. These men did things with other men sometimes in the very bathroom I was standing in despite the risk. My vocabulary increased with new and foreign words like blow-job, cock, cum, dick, and jack-off, words I filed away for future research.

Once I knew there were others like me, it became my quest to find them without drawing any attention to myself. My secret must never be discovered. The more I read, the more I learned about the unspoken code used by men who like men. The code included non-verbal signals like a foot softly tapping under the bathroom stall next to you, which meant the stranger there was "looking". The glance over at you from the urinal while standing far enough back to allow a view of the goods. The subtle adjusting of the crotch. The brief eye contact. The looking back to see if he was looking back.

I didn't know it at the time, but I was becoming a cruiser. What is a cruiser, you ask? Long before the internet, chat rooms, craigslist or apps like Grindr, gays found connections and sex through random, anonymous sexual encounters. These meetings usually happened in places like parks, gyms, public restrooms, department stores and mall restrooms. Cruising was especially common among men who couldn't risk being seen in a gay bar, adult bookstore, or with another man because of their occupation, wife, or reputation. I qualified on all counts. I was a conservative Baptist pastor, married to my wife raising three young children with a stellar reputation in my church communities.

I perfected the art of cruising over the years by making men my study. I studied their every move, their body language, their habits. I listened to their speech patterns. I watched what they watched. I took note if they took note of me or another man. I read every bathroom wall. I studied their bodies and watched for physical responses. I watched carefully for any sign that they might be like me. It didn't take long for me to begin to see the patterns. I learned that men like me were everywhere if you knew what to look for. I found them in the car next to me at an intersection, at church, at school, in the park, walking down the street, in the grocery store, at the gym, and in the mall. The language was mostly non-verbal. It usually started with a split-second-too-long eye contact or a casual adjustment of the crotch. It could include one too many shakes at the urinal, a foot tapping under a stall or being a bit too close when brushing by me. Driving through the park, it could be a couple of flashes of the brake lights from the car that just passed or a slight nod of the head while passing. In public, it was often a quick glance from the eyes to the crotch and back. This is the language of cruising which I learned to speak fluently.

By the time I was in my 30s, cruising was a part of my very being. I was subconsciously cruising all the time. Within a few hours in a new town, I could easily locate the most likely successful cruising spots like a pro. Once I found the hot spots, my highly refined gaydar alerted me to other men who were also looking for sex. Often it was as simple as spotting a man while walking through the mall - which is exactly what I was doing one Tuesday morning when a very handsome, muscular Puerto Rican arranging merchandise near the entrance of a store caught my attention. I saw him and he saw me. Our eye contact was brief but direct and full of the language of cruising. Instantly I knew I needed to stop in that store and examine the merchandise...him.

I casually wandered into the store and pretended to shop but I only had eyes for him. We locked eyes. He smiled and came over to see if I needed any help. I most certainly needed and wanted his help. I don't recall what conversation took place, but he assured me he was alone.

He then led me to a corner of the store, behind the always elaborate display of stuffed animals where he could keep an eye out for any customers who might wander in and my tall frame could be easily hidden while on my knees. I thought I hit the jackpot! As I drank in his muscles, bronze skin and growing bulge of his cock that he rubbed through his tight jeans while looking enticingly into my eyes.

With no words exchanged, he pushed me down to my knees behind the display, quickly unzipped his pants, and whipped out the most gorgeous, thickest, cock I had ever seen. My heart was beating out of my chest as I grabbed the thickness and wrapped my lips around it sucking it in ecstasy. He moaned quietly and pushed his cock deep into my throat making me gag. I wanted him - all of him - but as quickly as it began, he pulled away, zipped up and walked to the front of the store to greet a customer just coming in. I stood up, straightened myself and quickly resumed my shopping charade while I attempted to regain my composure. The adrenaline was still rushing through my veins. I waited around a bit longer hoping the store would clear out again so we could finish what we had begun, but to my disappointment, more shoppers strolled in. As I walked toward the exit I made a point to lock eyes with him and said, "Thank you". With a wink and a smile he replied, "No, thank you!"

Later that week I returned to the mall hoping to have another encounter. He saw me from inside the crowded store as I strolled by. His eyes lit up and he gave me a tiny knowing smile and that ever so slight nod of the head. I never saw him again after that day. I often wonder if we were caught on security cameras and he lost his job because of it. I'll never know who he was, but I think about him every time I pass by a Disney Store.

PRAYER

To self while looking in the mirror: 'You're disgusting. You're despicable. I hate you. You're worthless.'

CHAPTER 5
You Don't Care About Me

Because my marriage was a woven tapestry of codependency, there was no part of my life Dee wasn't a part of...except one. I worked very hard to keep that part from her. She knew I was seeing a counselor, but I led her to believe that this counselor was to help me deal with the stress of being in ministry. She understood at first.

I entered ex-gay therapy thinking my life was good with the exception of one small thing: my sexual sin. At the very first counseling session I asked, "I'm not going to have to tell my wife about this am I?" That was my worst fear. My hope was I could quietly get fixed and go on my merry way without my wife ever knowing. At my first counseling appointment I felt the sobering realization that my problem was not one part of me, it was me.

The counselor compassionately listened as I tearfully poured out my life story to him. For the first time in my life I was being completely honest with someone. At first it was a joyous relief to actually speak to life all that I had hidden within. With each visit to his office or email I peeled away more layers. The more layers I peeled the more were revealed. I began to understand the unhealthy life patterns I had formed in life. It became immediately apparent that my relationship with my wife was a codependent mess that required a dramatic makeover beginning with me. I very carefully made small changes in the way I operated in our marriage, but because our lives were so entwined those small tremors stirred the sleeping volcano warning me of a coming eruption.

I scrambled to downplay the cracks in our marriage revealed by the tremors. I tried to share just enough to satisfy her questions and stay far away from the real reason I was seeing a counselor. But I was changing. For the first time in my life I was feeling emotion. As I learned to feel, the flood gates opened and the tears flowed easily. My wife could not understand what was happening to her husband. Her marriage.

On this particular day, my wife had finally had enough of being left in the dark. She knew something was wrong - really wrong - but she didn't know what. She knew her husband was falling apart before her very eyes. She knew he had inexplicably shut her out of parts of his life with an order of "NO TRESPASSING". This was new. This was not how our relationship worked. We had always been one. She was hurt. She was confused. She was scared. The well-oiled gears of our marriage were jerking, skipping and grinding in foreign, frightening ways. Our conflict began in the living room when she demanded answers.

"What is going on with you?! I am your wife, I have a right to know!" She insisted.

I choked back the tears and tried to reassure her.

"I'm not ready to talk about this yet. I need you to leave me alone until I'm ready to talk." This only made matters worse. Her eyes widened in fear and her voice rose.

"What?! Now you're really scaring me. What is going on?! Are you having an affair? What is happening?"

I knew I needed to get out of her presence. I left the living room, attempting to escape into the basement where my makeshift office was. Before I could get to the basement she spun me around, backed me into the corner and again demanded, "Tell me what is going on! What is happening?!" I felt small and helpless, like a child in her presence. My world was crumbling and I knew it, yet I could do nothing about it. I was losing control. I felt panic taking over. Like an animal can sense fear, she could smell my fear and weakness. She was relentlessly determined to get answers. Answers I was not ready to provide.

I cowered in the corner, sobbing, unable to form coherent thoughts or words. The fight-or-flight instinct kicked in. I knew I had to break free. With her only inches away from my body, I opened the door behind me and stumbled down the stairs, eyes blurry from the tears streaming down my face. She continued to hurl the same questions over and over again.

"What is going on? Tell me what is happening!"

Halfway down, I collapsed on the steps and heard my own voice scream the words, "I just want somebody to care about me!"

My life was full of people who said they cared about me. My parents loved me. They provided a good life for me. I had two brothers and a sister who said they loved me. I had friends. I had a wife and three kids. I had ministry colleagues. There were many people in my life who, if they had heard my cry on the steps that night would have responded with a resounding, "But I DO care about you," which is exactly what my wife said. But her words were empty and meaningless. They annoyed me. Logically, I knew she thought she cared about me, but I didn't believe it. How could she possibly care when she didn't know me? No one knew the truth about me. I spent a lifetime making sure no one knew.

Being backed into the literal and figurative corner that day revealed the pressure cooker that was hissing and rattling inside me. The pressure was more than I could contain. The pain locked deep in the darkest recesses of my wounded heart and soul exploded into the light finding life for the very first time. At that moment it felt like death. Ready or not, my secret was coming out. My house of cards was crashing down.

In my heart I knew there was no turning back now. Soon everyone would know the truth about me. I was not who they thought I was. This terrified me.

It was no wonder I felt no one cared about me. I didn't care about myself. The concept of self-love was foreign to me. In fact, I was taught that to love yourself was sinful.

You are despicable. Disgusting. You make me sick, I often said to myself in the mirror as tears of guilt, shame, and anger streamed down my face. I hated the man I saw in the mirror. He let me down over and over again. He was weak. He was insufficient. He was a fraud. He was letting everyone down, they just didn't know it yet. These mirror conversations were increasing in frequency. I was convinced that if I could hate who I was it would motivate me to be someone else. Someone others could love.

The messages *You are not enough. Something is wrong with you. You are not worthy. There is nothing good in you. You are not to be trusted...*played on a constant loop in my head. I came by them honestly. This was the mantra of my parents and my church where I received my earliest teachings about myself.

"The heart is deceitfully wicked! Who can trust it?" the preacher quoted in a thundering voice from the pulpit. "Trust in the Lord with all your heart and don't trust your own understanding." I took to heart these messages. I did not trust myself. I sought the will of God in everything and assumed that whatever I wanted was the opposite of what God wanted. My parents backed up what the preachers said. You can do nothing good on your own. Any good in you is God shining through you. You are to deny self because self will always choose the wrong thing. You are to take no credit or praise. You are sinful. You are broken.

Am I broken? I asked my young self. *I don't feel broken, but something must be wrong with me because mom seems worried about me.* As early as 4 and 5 years old, Mom expressed concern about me being too "soft".

"Boys don't play with dolls!" she chided when she discovered I was playing with GI Joes at my best friend's house. I was four. The posable soldiers with all of their equipment infatuated me. My mother saw them as Barbies for boys, a sort of gateway doll to the feminine world of Barbie. Barbie's glamorous and colorful world did appeal to me, her stylish gowns, elegant dream house, the sleek, pink convertible, and of course her handsome, bronze-skinned, boyfriend Ken. I never objected when a friend suggested, "let's play with my Barbies!" My secret keeping began at a young age.

I reasoned that something must be wrong with me. "I wish there were more boys for Joel to play with, I'm concerned about him playing with girls all the time." She often mused out loud to my Dad. It was true. It just so happened that I was a minority among the children in the houses near me. Her concern was confusing to me because in my mind these children were simply my friends. It never occurred to me that they weren't boys.

Mom was always concerned about my lack of interest in stereotypical boy things like playing sports. Sports never held my interest. Competition and winning was not motivational to me. I was a creative. My vivid imagination kept me entertained for hours, creating worlds and scenes for my little toys, blocks, Hot Wheels and stuffed animals. Whether in the sandbox, the exposed maple tree roots, or making a tent from blankets and chairs, I was content with escaping into worlds of my own creation. My imagination was easily stirred. I loved my watercolors, magic markers, crayons, Play-Doh, and record player. The world was my playground and I was determined to to make the most of it. Ironically, it was that very interest in creativity and art that bound my mother and me together. She was a talented artist and found beauty everywhere in the world around her. She and I shared a passion for art, nature, music, cooking, and creating.

"Mom, Kim and I are putting on a show with Jill and our friends in her backyard!" I excitedly reported to her.

"Mom, Stacy has a playroom in her basement with a kitchen our size and a whole lot of toys! Can I go play with her?" Mom reluctantly agreed, but I could feel her concern. She knew.

"Aaron, take your brother to play ball today with you and your friends." She interrupted my stuffed animal parade on the front porch with these instructions to my older brother. Like any 12-year-old boy would do, he groaned, complained and strongly objected to dragging along his uninterested 6-year-old brother. I didn't want to go anymore than he wanted to take me along. I hoped mom would change her mind. But mom knew. She was on a mission to make a man out of me. She insisted that he take me with him and instructed him to involve me in the game.

I grabbed a stuffed animal, or Hot Wheel car and followed behind him at a suitable distance to the park where his friends were already playing catch. Once at the field, I was happy to be ignored by the older boys while I sat in the soft grass making clover chains, staring at the clouds till they became animals, and picking bouquets of dandelions to present to my mother when we arrived home. It was an ideal, unspoken agreement between my brother and me. I would go along to appease my mother, and he would not make me play ball with his friends.

"Gerald, why don't you take Joel down to your workshop and teach him how to build something?" Mom would urge my dad. I liked the prospect of doing creating something with Dad, but he we went about things very differently. He reveled in the details while I was inspired by the big picture. I grew impatient with the measuring and cutting while he grew impatient with my perceived lack of interest. He would eventually get angry because I wasn't paying attention, and I would wander off to more interesting things in the basement while he finished the project without me.

I was the youngest of four children. My siblings were six, ten and twelve years older than me. They were all athletically inclined, except me. They bonded with Dad over sports while I bonded with mom over creativity.

What is wrong with me? I wondered. *Why is mom so concerned about me?* I had no answers. I learned to feign interest in "boy things" enough to make mom feel better about me being "normal".

My parents were on an increasingly narrow road of expressing their faith. My mother stopped wearing pants and all but a tiny bit of makeup. My father determined that the King James Bible was the only true Bible. The house was cleaned out of any rock and roll records. We were forbidden to listen to most popular music. Our home was filled with Christian music, hymns and classical works. We got rid of our TV and stopped celebrating Halloween and Easter. We no longer went swimming. I was never allowed to wear shorts, go shirtless or even wear a tank top. Movies, plays, or anything in a theatre was off limits. Most fiction books were replaced with biographies of famous missionaries and preachers. We went to church twice on Sunday, and several other times throughout the week.

Eventually my parents decided the Southern Baptist churches were becoming too liberal, so we began attending the much more conservative and cult-like independent, fundamental Baptist churches. This is when I began to feel deeply that no one cared about me. I learned that while the church said "everyone's welcome" what they meant was everyone's welcome to come and be just like us. When the preacher said "Come just as you are" what he really meant was come as you are, come just as you are but you better not stay that way. When they said "we're all sinners" what they really meant was we're all sinners but your sin is the worst of all sins and you'll be labeled, limited, and looked down on forever.

Even when people claim to care about you, it doesn't feel like they do when they demand you show up as who they want and need, not as yourself. I knew I would never be celebrated for who I was as a human being. I quickly learned that the core of me, what I loved the most had to be invisible.

This is not just for LGBTQ people. This feeling happens in all types of families when spoken and unspoken expectations are placed upon a person who has zero interest or desire in being whatever the other person has in mind for them. We all can fall victim to thinking that family or the people we love owe us to be what we want them to be rather than who they genuinely are.

Unconditional love doesn't come with strings attached.

Me in my A.C.E. Christian School Uniform at age 13 when my body REALLY began changing! I was already 6 ft tall in this photo.

PRAYER

"God, please forgive me for thinking bad thoughts about Rob, Mike, John, Larry, Steve, Tim, and Paul...oh, and Dale...and...Chris...and..."

CHAPTER 6
The Sex Mis-education of Joel

In 1977 when I was 11, we moved to Effingham, Illinois and my parents enrolled me in the tiny Christian school in the basement of the small church we began attending. The school was part of the nationwide movement of churches starting Christian schools to protect the next generation from the secular, humanistic, evolution-teaching, public schools that were corrupting children and encouraging them to attend state universities where they would only be further encouraged to question beliefs, study science, and think for themselves. Public schools were the new enemy. Christian schools were popping up everywhere as an alternative.

I went to an ACE (Accelerated Christian Education) school which was modeled after the concept of a one-room school house where all the grades studied together. It was an exceptionally ineffective, self-study curriculum where all the students sat quietly in cubicles facing the wall around the perimeter of a large open room in the basement of the Church. In keeping with the rising popularity of God and Country themes of the late 70s through early 80s, everything was painted red, white, and blue. There was no teacher but adult supervisors were available to help with questions when a student raised the little Christian or American flag at their cubicle. My sister, who had an elementary education degree was the only somewhat qualified teacher in the room. I spent 3 years in that ACE school and learned very little except how to memorize the answers to the test long enough to go to the testing station and successfully retake the test I had failed moments earlier.

I had quietly begun puberty a year earlier. No one seemed to notice and if they did, no one said anything. By the time I was twelve, hair began to sprout in new places and I noticed the same on the other boys my age and older. I studied their growing, changing bodies. I looked forward to the locker room where I took mental snapshots to add to my image database. I captured every line of their muscles, every hair on their body, and every bulge in their briefs. I memorized them. I replayed them over and over again at home in the shower with soap or in my bedroom with Jergens lotion or Vaseline. When that ran out I desperately attempted one and only one painful use of Vicks Vapor Rub.

It was also in Effingham where I learned those like me were ridiculed, hated, and feared. Looking back, I now realize that the first gay pride parades were happening around the USA at that time which explains why homosexuality was becoming such a common topic from the pulpit. "Those Sodomites are out in the streets wearing practically nothing at all, parading their perversion unashamedly. They are flaunting their sinful abominations in the face of God. It's a modern Sodom and Gomorrah right here in the United States. If God doesn't destroy them soon, he'll have to apologize to Sodom and Gomorrah." the preacher would lament.

For a young, closeted gay boy in puberty listening to the pastor describe throngs of half-naked men in the streets of San Francisco doing unspeakable things in public, it was a real turn on! I sat in the church pew engrossed by the preacher's words while imagining the scene he described. From my tiny, sleepy town of Effingham it was hard for me to believe that in another part of the US there were naked men parading in public ... but now my interest and penis were aroused. I had no idea what unspeakable things the preacher referred to, yet I wanted to know more. As I listened intently week after week I learned that the men who "did things" with men were called homosexuals or gays, but from the pulpit they were called queers, Sodomites, perverts, pedophiles, sissies, reprobates, faggots and of course, abominations. "They want to be called gay, but gay means happy and there's no way they can be happy while living in sin, so we refuse to call them gay." the preacher bellowed. I learned that we were to mock, shame, and reject those queers in the severest of ways. "They should be stoned!" "Homosexuality is the unpardonable sin! God hates their perversion! The Bible tells us that it is an abomination for a man to lie with another man. It is vile and evil. God will surely judge them for their sin and they will burn forever in hell." It was common for some form of these themes to pop up in fiery sermons nearly every Sunday.

"God has given them over to a reprobate mind and they cannot be saved." "God has a special place in hell reserved for their kind." I didn't know what a reprobate was, but it sure didn't sound good. Later, when the AIDS crisis hit I heard, "They should all be shipped off to an island where they can infect themselves with disease and die." The hatred was palpable. As if the hate itself wasn't enough, it was often accompanied by the preachers mocking and imitating effeminate men. As they bellowed and spewed their hate, they pranced around the stage with limp wrists and talked with a lisp. Some of the crowd laughed. Others shook their heads in disgust. And some shouted a hearty "Amen!" or "That's right!" as the preacher mocked and warned of God's condemnation and inevitable judgement.

I learned that homosexuals were infiltrating schools in an effort to "recruit" children to be gay. As far as the church was concerned, homosexuality and pedophilia went hand in hand. Fearful parents pulled their children closer to them as preachers warned that homosexuals were out to get their children. I wasn't exactly sure what any of this really meant, but I sensed I was one of them. If anyone ever found out, I'd receive the same mocking, shaming and hatred.

When I heard the words "homosexual" or "gay" I could feel the loathing attached to them. I knew they had something to do with forbidden sex, but I really didn't understand what it all meant since any type of sex education was non-existent in my world. I resolved to do my own research and learn more. My research began with the very old and thick dictionary on our living room bookshelves. First, I looked up the word gay. To my surprise it meant "Happy or excited". This perplexed me. Why is that a bad thing? I like being happy and excited. There must be more to this.

I flipped the pages to find homosexual and homosexuality. I stared at the words leaping off the page to me: "a person, usually a man, who is sexually attracted to people of the same sex. Sexual activity with another of the same sex."

Hmm, I know sex is naughty and we don't talk about it, but this also includes something about men having sex with men. Is that what I am? A homosexual? No, it can't be. I don't even know what sex is. I'm just thinking the wrong thoughts about boys. I need to stop touching myself and thinking of them like that.

Yet reading these words made me feel a little naughty, excited and aroused. I needed to know more. My next stop was the set of outdated encyclopedia-type books in boxes in our basement. They seemed antique to me, but I remembered that one volume was about human development or something similar. I figured that might get me closer to some useful information. I thumbed through the pages until I found some vintage, health class type photos and drawings accompanying articles about puberty and the body changes boys and girls could anticipate. I quickly skipped past the uninteresting section about girls' bodies and found the part about boys. "Around the age of 14 or 15 boys will notice their bodies changing." I felt proud that I was ahead of schedule. I was already growing tall and hair had appeared around my penis in the 5th grade. In the book I learned (in very clinical terms) about such things as puberty and pubic hairs ... but it was something called nocturnal emissions that really stopped me in my tracks. *What?! This says I might have a nocturnal emission? What is that?! Why didn't anyone tell me? I don't even know what either of those words mean. If this is going to happen to me, I need to know what that is.* Going back to the dictionary I looked up the word "nocturnal".

noc·tur·nal

/näk'tərnl/

adjective

done, occurring, or active at night.

"most owls are nocturnal"

Hmm so it happens at night, but what is it that happens at night? I flipped to the E section of the dictionary and found the word "emissions".

e·mis·sion

/ə'miSH(ə)n/

plural noun: emissions

the production and discharge of something, especially gas or radiation.

"the effects of lead emission on health"

You've got to be kidding me! Some like gas or radiation might come out of me at night?! I turned back to the encyclopedia to read more but the obscure words there provided very little more insight.

I skimmed over the rest - enough to learn that it didn't seem to be anything I should be concerned about - and closed the book. I tried to put it out of my mind and figured I would know a nocturnal emission if I encountered one. I was in college before I learned that nocturnal emissions were simply wet dreams ... something I never experienced, probably because I had plenty of self-induced, daytime emissions. After I exhausted the small collection of outdated encyclopedias, I turned to the National Geographic magazines. I poured over the images of humans from around the world who seemed to always be wearing far less than we did in America. There were lots of boobs and butts, but very few penises except on naked little boys playing in mud puddles in the jungle. These images bored me so I turned to the public library. I started in the children's section and found an assortment of books about this new word "puberty". The books were written in plain language I could understand with accompanying drawings and even some photos. Jackpot! This was what I wanted. I excitedly read, while occasionally looking over my shoulder to make sure no one was watching. I was thrilled to learn that my body was going to be changing even more than it already was. Several books had drawings of boys in various stages of puberty showing their muscles forming, hair growing in new places, bodies getting taller, and genitals growing larger in each pic.

Now this is exciting! I wonder how big mine will get? I often compared my body in the mirror to the boys pictured in the book at the library. I memorized the drawings of flaccid and erect penises - especially the ones that showed the size I could expect my penis to achieve over the next few years. I dared not check out the book for fear my parents would find it and forbid me from visiting the library. It wasn't long before I exhausted the few books in the children's section of the library and wondered what I might find over in the adult section.

One day I finally got up the courage to explore this foreign territory of the library. I wasn't even sure where to begin, so I decided to start with the H section of the card catalogue. Keeping an eye over my shoulder for any nosey people, I found home, then homo, then homogenous, and eventually homosexual. To my shock there were many cards there representing many books, both non-fiction and fiction, that were about homosexuality. My body quivered from the adrenaline rush fueled by my discovery. I glanced around to see if anyone was watching me before grabbing a piece of paper and one of those tiny eraserless pencils the library kept nearby for just this purpose. I scribbled as many of the numbers down as I could. I didn't dare write the titles for fear someone would see what I was about to go searching for.

Shoving the drawer back in place, I stuffed the paper in my pocket and disappeared into the long line of tall bookshelves looking for the letters and numbers scribbled on my paper. My heart beat faster when the numbers began getting closer to matching the ones I held in my hand. When the word homosexuality jumped off the spine of a book, I realized I was in the right place.

My eyes scanned the titles lined up on the shelf. I couldn't believe what I was seeing. It was a goldmine of forbidden literature. Thanks to the Effingham Public Library, my sex education had officially begun. Over the next months and years, I spent hours pouring over these books learning new words and terms related to sexuality and sex. The more I read, the more I learned and the broader my search became. I found books like *The Joy of Gay Sex* with photographs, provocative images, and detailed descriptions of what men did together in bed. I learned that homoeroticism could be found in art and photography books about the human form, workout and fitness books, and in a large variety of magazines in the reading room. The ads in the back of some particularly provocative mens exercise magazines were especially titillating. I discovered gay anthologies and historical accounts of gay life. I can still recall some of the stories I read in the collections of short stories entitled *Men On Men*. For a small, midwest town in Illinois, I now realize they had a surprisingly large collection of these materials. I'd like to thank the unknown librarian responsible for my sex education.

With each piece of information I learned, I realized I was the homosexual that the preachers screamed about. It was the beginning of living in fear of someone finding out about me. Shame was the perfect companion for my fear. Shame and fear quickly took up an ever-increasing residence in my life. I kept reading. The more I read, the more shame I felt for being who I was and the fear of being discovered multiplied.

Despite all the turmoil growing inside me, I was a good boy. I wasn't rebellious. I was compliant. I read my Bible and prayed every day. I memorized lengthy passages of scripture. I respected and obeyed my parents. I didn't cause anyone any trouble. Adults always commented on what a nice boy I was. I was well-liked, but I liked boys. I knew that if anyone discovered that, I would no longer be liked. I would be shunned, condemned and mocked. I might even be sent away to a home for troubled boys somewhere far away. No one must ever know.

I dedicated my life to being who my parents and the church taught me that God wanted me to be. I truly wanted that, mostly because I thought it would change that "other" part of me that no one knew about. The Church told me that the more I surrendered to God, the more like Him I would become and find joy and fulfillment in serving Him. I was willing to do this.

I spent sixth, seventh, and eighth grade in the pitiful little Christian school run by our church. Despite the poor education, I am a socially extroverted person so I made friends easily. Because the school was small, all the boys in the school were on the basketball team - including me - even though I had no idea what I was doing. I hated sports, but by eighth grade my body was changing rapidly and I was already six foot tall...so everyone expected me to not only like and play the game, but to also excel at it. The only plus side was that when we played other teams I got to drink in the hint of a bulge beneath their short shorts and sometimes more in the locker room. The game didn't interest me, but the players did.

The summer before I was to enter my freshman year of high school, my parents got upset with the church we were attending and decided we wouldn't attend there anymore nor would I remain enrolled in the church school. My social life abruptly ended as my parents cut off all contact with anyone from that church or school. Suddenly I was completely alone. When the school year rolled around that fall, they decided to take the unprecedented move of homeschooling me rather than put me in the humanistic public school system. And so began four of the most isolated, miserable years of my life. I had no friends and no social life. The piano became my only friend. I studied in confinement and boredom. My parents had no business homeschooling me, but that didn't deter them. Because homeschooling was a new and foreign concept, they feared being reported to the authorities so they required me to stay inside and study out of view of the neighbors until the other schools released their students for the day. I hated every day of this prison.

As soon as the school day was over I would ride my bike all over town, making sure to stop by the public high school to watch the track and field team practice. I studied the shirtless boys in their flimsy shorts, hoping to catch sight of more skin than they intended to show. I imagined their bodies naked. By the time I got home, I was so worked up that I convinced myself that if I could just masturbate this one last time it would allow me to put the images behind me once and for all and everything would be different here on out.

That was the last time God. I won't do it again. I will be godly now. I'm so sorry. Please forgive me.

I continued to consume all the related books at the library and expanded my search to mens style and workout books. They usually had what I now realize were quite homoerotic images to illustrate the style and exercise they claimed to be about. One large, coffee table book was filled with homoerotic images of men used to illustrate each workout. I checked it out and consulted it often for my workouts which only involved my right hand. It was my porn. In the magazine section of the library I discovered the same. I devoured celebrity magazines, fitness magazines, and mens style and fashion classics like GQ. Basically, if there was an attractive man on the cover of the magazine - I looked at it.

Because of my height people often assumed I was much older than I was. I used this to my advantage. I learned that if I acted older, people assumed I must be and they had no reason to be suspicious of me. About once a month my parents would decide to drive to Mattoon, Illinois which was about thirty miles away. Mattoon was slightly larger than Effingham and had a small mall with stores like Sears and K-Mart that we didn't have. It was there that I discovered Waldenbooks. Each trip, my plan was to spend a bit of time shopping with my parents in Sears or K-Mart until I grew bored. I asked their permission to go exploring on my own and meet back with them at a designated hour. They trusted me and always agreed to the arrangement. I casually sauntered away until out of their view and then made a bee-line for Waldenbooks in the main mall. Once inside, I would casually peruse the extensive magazine collection, working my way closer and closer to the top shelf area at the far end of the long rack where the adult magazines peeked out from behind the fashion and style collection. With a LIFE magazine in my hand, I feigned interest while glancing at the forbidden titles above me: Playboy, Gallery, Penthouse. None of the big-haired, big-breasted women on the covers of these magazines interested me in any way. I could still recall the Playboy my cousins showed me once and all I could think was *Eww! Why are all these women naked and why would anyone want to look at that?!*

But it wasn't Playboy I sought, it was Playgirl! Somewhere along the way, I learned there was a magazine that had pictures of naked men in it. Now THAT was something I wanted to see! I glanced around me to make sure the store clerk and no one else was watching as I stealthily grabbed the magazine and stuck it between the pages of the oversized LIFE magazine in my hands. My heart raced from the naughty risk I was taking as well as what my eyes were about to see. As nonchalantly as I could, I strolled to the photography section in the back of the store. This was by design. The photography books were usually large, coffee table, size books which made the magazines easier to hide between pages. I also figured it wouldn't be considered unusual for a young teenager to be exploring the topic of photography.

Positioning myself with my back to the rear of the store where I could see anyone who might be headed in my direction, I opened the magazine with shaking hands. The images inside the magazine took my breath away. I consumed details, memorizing them for future reference. Page after page, there were men in various stages of undress or completely nude. Some were famous actors or stars while others were everyday men with a short bio about their interests and career. It didn't matter to me who they were or what they did. I didn't read the articles. I just wanted to see the goods. I memorized the images, left the magazine in the photography book and casually returned to the magazine rack to replace the LIFE magazine and exit the store. Thanks to our monthly excursions to Mattoon, I rarely missed an issue of Playgirl magazine in my teen years.

At age thirteen, I hit a rapid growth spurt that stopped when I reached six feet five inches at age fifteen. My parents couldn't keep me in clothing that fit. I outgrew everything as fast as I got into it. I grew self-conscious of my pant legs and sleeves always being too short for my long body. I grew so fast that my body didn't have time to adjust, so I was clumsy. Hair was growing on my face and body. But thanks to my dedicated extensive research at the library and Walden Books, I now understood what this puberty thing was all about. While my understanding of sex wasn't exactly accurate, I had read enough to have a basic understanding of both heterosexual and homosexual sex. I didn't spend much time on the heterosexual descriptions because they held no interest to me. And since my parents seemed oblivious to anything other than my height, I taught myself about sex. And how to shave my lip and chin, treat the pimples appearing on my face, wear deodorant, and attempt to style my too-short conservatively cut hair.

I suppose the lack of any acknowledgement of my transition from child to teenager (despite all the outward signs) was why I was surprised the day my Dad came into my room and said he wanted to talk to me. Somehow, I knew what was about to happen the moment he entered. *Oh, no Dad, not this. Please don't tell me you're going to do "the talk" with me now?!* But my fears were correct. Nervously, he sat down on my bed next to me and began his rehearsed speech. Like all proper speeches it had an introduction, a body and a conclusion. It went like this:

Introduction: "Son, I just wanted you to know that you may notice your body changing."

It was hard for me not to roll my eyes at this revelation. This was definitely not news to me. I didn't dare respond, but inside I said, *You mean more than this?! I'm a six-foot five-inch tall fifteen year-old who wears a size thirteen shoe. Yeah, I've noticed.*

I wondered why Dad was warning me of coming changes, when he had not noticed the very obvious-to-me changes such as the hairs on my chin and upper lip - of which I was embarrassed and proud. I found Bic disposable razors in the bathroom drawer and painfully dry shaved my face as they appeared. I had certainly noticed the few straggling hairs on my chest and the little "happy trail" leading from my belly button down to my penis ... which seemed to be growing larger every week (it did finally stop growing at the very impressive size of – wouldn't you like to know-and-a-half inches). I had noticed my own body odor and the need for deodorant. I had noticed the hair on my legs, arms, and butt. I noticed the curl that appeared in my normally straight hair. I wanted to shout, *You haven't noticed any of this?!* but I also wanted this "talk" to be over as quickly as possible so I just listened.

Following Dad's brilliant introduction came the body of the speech, which as I expected was going to be the really juicy part where we talked about sex. I waited in curiosity, wondering what he would say. While I absentmindedly stared at the floor, he awkwardly said: "And son, you might get an erection. If you do, don't worry about it. It will go away." I waited for more, but that was it. That was the entire body of his speech. There was no explanation about what an erection was, but of course, I was well acquainted with them at this point. He was right, I did get one, often. He was also right that they would go away. They did go away. I could make them disappear with the magic of my hands once, twice, three times, sometimes four or five times a day. He was right. After they came, they disappeared ... until the next one.

Dad concluded his speech with the simple closing line: "If you have any questions, let me know." *Oh Dad, if you only knew how many questions I used to have and how much work I went through to answer them. Oh, I know Dad. You have no idea how much I know.*

I mumbled, "Okay Dad." He seemed satisfied with our talk and didn't wait around for any questions. He left the room and I closed the door feeling amused and disappointed. I have a feeling he went back to my Mom and said, "Janet, I finally talked with Joel about ... you know." and she probably said, "Oh good! I'm glad. So, how did it go?" I imagine my Dad stood tall and proud and said, "It went well. We had a good talk and I think he understands now."

In my room, I grabbed the lotion and the JCPenney's catalogue and turned to the mens underwear section in an effort to find something to distract me from the awkward speech my Dad had just delivered. I was grateful for my self-developed literacy, my ability to look older than I was in public and to be able to successfully hide the truth of my desires. Books and magazines continued to be a source of my joy and truth-seeking about the body, my curiosities and desires.

Take the dearest things to me
If that's how it must be to draw me closer to You
Let my disappointments come
Lonely days without the sun
If in sorrow more like You I'll become

I'll trade sunshine for rain, comfort for pain
That's what I'll be willing to do
For whatever it takes for my will to break
That's what I'll be willing to do
That's what I'll be willing to do

- Lanny Wolfe, Whatever It Takes

PRAYER

"I want to surrender to you, God. I'll do whatever you want me to do...even if it means going to Russia."

CHAPTER 7
Full-Time Christian Service

More than anything, I wanted to be used by God (yes, that's the phrase we used). Being godly was my goal in life. It was an undefinable goal, but I assumed I'd know when I hit it. I never did. No one could really explain what godly would look like on a person. It was just one of those characteristics that people used to describe someone they perceived to be godly mostly because they weren't aware of any ungodly characteristics about them. For example: it was easy to assume the kind, little old lady who attended church in her Sunday best with her well-worn Bible in hand every time the doors were open must be godly, right? The missionaries who sacrificed so much to take the Gospel to foreign lands...surely they must be godly. The well-known preachers who built large ministries and delivered fiery sermons that motivated throngs of people to make decisions for Christ... obviously they were godly since God was using them so visibly. My parents were considered godly because they just looked and acted the part - but as a child, I wondered if the church knew my parents the way I knew them... would it still think of them as godly?

Probably not. It was always confusing when word got out that someone previously considered godly was caught in some unacceptable sin and immediately labeled ungodly or maybe even unsaved. Since we were taught that all of us were sinners and God hates sin, then how was anyone ever to be godly? There was a definite ranking of sins. You could have a serious problem with pride or lust. As long as no one knew, it didn't seem to impact your godliness quotient at all. In fact, you could even acknowledge your struggles in a prayer request or testimony in church and you'd be lauded for your honesty and humility. But if you admitted to even having a homosexual thought, you'd never be viewed the same in the church and certainly wouldn't be labeled godly. Even as a young boy I saw through all of this and wondered how good I had to be to be considered godly and how bad was "too bad" to remove that label? I wanted to question the logic behind this mystery, but questions like that were frowned upon ... so I just kept on trying to surrender to God and follow his ways, never quite sure if I was doing enough or not.

My Dad required us to wear a tie to all church meetings and a suit jacket on Sundays. I hated the binding noose around my neck, but I wore it as instructed. Everyone in the family carried a Bible to church. We always sat within the front three rows of the sanctuary. I paid close attention to the sermons, took copious notes in my Bible, and highlighted or underlined important verses. A well-worn, marked-up Bible was another sign of the closeness of one's relationship to Christ. During the week I read my Bible every day and spent time praying on my knees. *God I only want to be what you want me to be. I want to be pleasing to you. I want to serve you. I want to be used by you.* It was with an honest and sincere heart that I regularly prayed this sentiment to God. I played the piano and sang duets with my Mom in church. My family was in church Sunday morning, Sunday night, Wednesday night, Thursday night visitation (which meant going door-to-door in our town asking people, "If you died today do you know where'd spend eternity?") and sometimes Saturday mornings for other church-related activities. I obeyed my parents and didn't cause anyone any trouble. I was well-liked - especially by the adults - and I was considered a good, godly boy. I liked the praise and approval of the adults in my life. It made me feel like I was doing something very right despite what they didn't know about me. Dare I say, I took pride in living up to this expectation?

These young and impressionable years of my life coincided with the 1970s coming to a close and the 1980s being ushered in. Christianity was becoming political. Being godly not only included what was done in the personal and church lives of a Christian but also included how one would show up in the world as a warrior for Christ. Jerry Falwell's "Moral Majority" was in full swing and rallied evangelicals around political issues. According to the preachers in our churches, the attack on Christianity was at an all-time high. Immorality and godlessness was running rampant in our nation following the sexual revolution and humanism of the 1960s and 1970s. Communism was threatening the world. America was forsaking God and if something didn't change, God would forsake America. The new enemies of the church were feminism, gay rights, abortion, and rock and roll. Pop culture was ruining our children and homes. Public schools and state universities were contributing to the moral decay of our nation. America was going to experience the judgement of God if Christians didn't stand up and start doing something.

Missions Conferences and Bible Conferences were annual events at many churches. The spirit of God seemed to move "mightily" in these. Missionaries would come and present a slide show of the far off land to which they were called. To a young boy in central Illinois, the colorful strange landscapes, rugged villages, odd looking creatures, unusual foods and people who looked different from me were quite fascinating. I looked forward to every missionary presentation. Scattered through the images were maps, demographics and statistics about how many unchurched people lived there who had never heard the Gospel of Jesus Christ. The congregation was reminded that the blood of these people would be on their hands at the day of judgement if they didn't send missionaries to reach these godless peoples. Every slide show ended with a photo of a beautiful sunset over a body of water or mountain, accompanied by a sad, emotionally manipulative song about people dying without Christ and the never-gets-old Bible verse known as "The Great Commission".

Go ye therefore, and teach all nations, baptizing them in the name of the Father, and of the Son, and of the Holy Ghost: Teaching them to observe all things whatsoever I have commanded you: and, lo, I am with you always, even unto the end of the world. Amen.

Tremendous emphasis was placed upon the callings of God in fundamental, independent Baptist churches. We were told that the world's population was growing faster than missionaries could keep up with. We were also told that fewer and fewer Christian young people were going to mission fields and this was due to their failure to answer God's call, not God's failure to call. We were reminded often of the words, "many are called...but few are chosen," and "here am I Lord ... send me." These words struck fear in my young heart.

Some of the missionaries told us about Christians in communist countries being captured, tortured, and sometimes killed for their refusal to stop preaching the Gospel. These "martyrs" were praised. Their sacrificial lives were held up to us as examples of the ultimate service to God. In Christian school I read, "God's Smuggler", the true story of Brother Andrew, a missionary well known for his risky and dangerous exploits smuggling Bibles into communist countries. Poorly produced Christian movies like *A Thief In the Night, The Burning Hell,* and *A Distant Thunder* gave me literal, spine-chilling nightmares. I would repeatedly ask God to save me during AND after the movies just in case I wasn't really saved the first time. The fear of being left behind after the rapture scared the hell out of me, which is what the movies were designed to do.

I still recall the disturbing photographs I saw in missionary slide shows and movies. One image in particular is forever stamped in my mind: it was a series of photographs of dead bodies stacked on a flatbed truck, followed by marching armies, tanks, and blindfolded Christians just before their death. The dramatic music climaxed with the final image of splattering blood on the screen. I was much too young to be terrorized by these images and messages. I didn't understand them. I only knew that it seemed that serving God meant horrible things.

We also heard stories from missionaries about people being imprisoned and even put to death for their faith. Russia in particular was a looming threat to be feared by every American. Because of the dismal education I was receiving at the tiny Christian school, my geography was always a blur. I wasn't sure where all these places were in the world, so communist country was the catch-all descriptor for every place I feared. Whether it was Romania, Russia, the Berlin Wall, or the Iron Curtain, I only knew I wanted to stay as far away from those scary places as possible if I valued my life.

Somewhere along the way, my family met Harlan Popov. He was a Bulgarian pastor who spent thirteen years in a prison camp for preaching the Gospel. His book "Tortured for his Faith" was an account of being arrested, imprisoned, and tortured for preaching the Gospel in his country. His story terrified me, but I looked up to him as a true hero of the faith. He became a family friend and often stayed in our home when he passed through. I didn't know where Bulgaria was, but it sounded Russian to me and that was all I needed to know to fear it. He was a weathered, skinny, old man who spoke with a thick accent. He sat at our dinner table while my parents sat in awe and respect of all that he represented. He was held in high esteem in our family. His stories of imprisonment and torture impacted me deeply and filled me with even greater fear that God would require the same of me if I were ever to be used of Him.

The pastors, missionaries and traveling evangelists warned us that if we didn't know and follow the will of God our lives would be doomed to misery and despair. Cautionary tales were told of unnamed people who didn't follow the will of God and instead made one wrong turn and their life ended up a complete mess - all because they didn't do what God had called them to do. "Put your all on the altar today and surrender to Him", they implored.

All of this confused me. On one hand we were told the stories of Christians who suffered great loss -

even imprisonment - when they were tortured for their faith while serving God ... which sure sounded like misery and despair to me. On the other hand, we were told that if we wanted to be happy and fulfilled we needed to surrender to the will of God ... which in my mind was likely to include being sent to dangerous lands and ending up being tortured in prison. The mixed messages were never explained, and we were discouraged from questioning God's perfect will. Instead, it was all covered by the encouragement to simply "surrender your all to God" and "trust God." Only then would you know true peace and joy.

Meanwhile, I was learning to play the piano and sing. I loved music and was pretty good at it. A dream was beginning to form that maybe one day I could either teach and/or perform, but as quickly as I began to dream I realized that this was what Joel wanted. And whatever Joel wanted was probably not what God wanted. My desires had to be sacrificed on the altar of God's will if I was ever going to be used by Him. This made me sad. I was left alone to contemplate these life choices. No one looked beneath the nice boy Joel to notice the internal conflict or to offer help. Similar to my puberty, I was left alone to figure it out.

Every church service ended with what was called an "invitation". While the pianist softly played, "I Surrender All," or "Just As I Am" the pastor, in a soft, imploring tone would begin inviting us all to make some sort of decision for Christ based on what we had just heard and seen.

"Every head bowed. Every eye closed. No one looking around. If you're here tonight and God has spoken to you, would you raise your hand please? No one is looking." Through squinted eyes, I looked to see if others were raising their hand because I didn't want to be the only one.

"Thank you, I see those hands. All over the auditorium hands are going up. Praise God. The Holy Spirit is certainly with us and speaking to us tonight. Maybe you're a young man who God is calling to preach or to be a missionary. Won't you surrender to God and come down and let one of us pray with you? God is speaking to you. Come now as we stand and sing 'I Surrender All'." If no one came forward to pray or make a decision, it meant that the invitation would go on much longer to allow God to work in hearts until decisions were made. Then the congregation would sing another verse of the song. At the end, the pastor would once again ask everyone to close their eyes, and again he would beg and plead and warn of the dangers of not listening to God and responding to him.

"You might walk out of here tonight and get hit by a car and it will be too late. Don't put it off. Today is the day of salvation." Then he'd address those like myself; "Now, I saw those hands that went up tonight that said, 'Pastor, God is speaking to me about something.' Don't delay. Come now. You'll be miserable until you surrender to God. Won't you come?"

I didn't feel God calling me to anything, but I did feel like I should probably surrender my fear of strange lands, prison and torture, and tell God I was willing to do whatever he wanted - even if that meant giving up my music dreams. This is what a good, godly boy should do, right? Plus, it might help me overcome my "problem" which was becoming increasingly more clear to me. I liked boys and that meant I was gay. The conflict was that I also liked God. A lot. I was doing everything I knew to be godly and I was godly ... except I was also gay and despite my most sincere efforts, I couldn't seem to not be gay. I knew my surrender to God would be a huge, next step of doing the right thing. I hoped that the more right I did, the less gay I would be because God would honor my heart and I would find my complete fulfillment in serving him.

It was with this reasoning that I began a life of believing that lie. For decades I kept believing the lie that the next godly thing I did would change who I was. "When I go to Bible college, I will change because I'll be in a good Christian environment with all these other young people who are also there to serve the Lord." "When I start dating girls, that will change my desires." When I get married, that will change my desires." "When I go into ministry, that will change me." When I have children, that will change me." "When I start my own church, that will change me." and the lies went on and on and on.

But I was an immature eleven-year-old boy and very alone in my journey. No one knew my internal struggle. So, it was at the end of a special service one night following a moving slide show by a missionary from Germany when I had the following conversation with myself during the invitation: *Joel if you're ever going to be happy and used by God you're going to have to surrender everything even if it means your dreams of music. You can't hold back from God. It's about what He wants, not what you want.* I knew I had no option but to surrender my all to God. All of this was swirling chaotically in my mind as the pianist played yet another verse of *I Surrender All* and the pastor pleaded desperately for decisions to be made. Finally, I summoned up the courage to silently say to God, *I don't know what you want me to do, but I'm willing to do it even if that means you want to send me to Russia as an undercover missionary to smuggle Bibles into communist countries. I know this means I'll probably end up in a prison camp somewhere being tortured and maybe killed, but if that's what you want from me, I'm willing. I just want to do whatever it is you want me to do.* I wasn't at all happy about this prospect, but I knew at least I would be remembered as someone who had given all to God and I would be honored and respected for it. Maybe someone would even write a book about my self-sacrifice, commitment to God's will and ultimate martyrdom. My parents had always expressed extreme admiration and reverence for missionaries, especially those who suffered great loss or death. To them, the greater the sacrifice, the greater the reward in heaven. Our home was full of books that told these stories. I knew that if I wanted to have the highest approval from my parents and God, my life needed to be one of great sacrifice. I decided I was willing to risk it.

With as much resolve as an eleven-year-old boy can muster up, I stepped out of my pew, walked down the aisle of the church, and met the assistant pastor waiting there (who later married my sister and became my brother-in-law).

"I just want to tell God that I'm willing to do whatever He wants me to do." I heard my shaking voice tell him. We knelt at the front pew and he prayed with me. I don't remember what he prayed, but I felt better for acknowledging and confronting my fear. *There, I said it. I am willing to do His will, no matter what that might be.* I shuddered at the thought of what might be next now that I had said these words. In my mind God was smiling down on me, but the smile seemed more ominous than approving. I imagined Him chuckling while rubbing his hands together in a now-I've-got-you-where-I-want-you! kind of way. The next thing I knew, I was standing in front of the congregation as the pastor announced to the congregation: "Joel has come forward to surrender to full-time Christian service." The men in the room said, "Amen!" and "Praise the Lord!" The women smiled approvingly and dabbed at the tears forming in the corners of their eyes. Inside I panicked. *Wait, I did what? I didn't say that. Is that what it meant? But...I didn't mean...but everyone seems so pleased with me. I guess that's what I did but I just didn't know that's what I did. What does this mean?* I wanted to blurt out a correction to the pastor. "No! wait! That's not what I said. That's not what I meant." But who was I to correct the pastor? He was the authority, God's anointed, the head of the church. He must know what he's talking about, right? I knew better than to argue with my elders. I smiled weakly at the congregation through misty eyes as I mentally reviewed the few minutes prior to this announcement. I knew what I said to the assistant pastor who met me at the front of the church. I knew I had not uttered the words "full-time Christian service" but that's what the pastor was saying now and there was no going back.

After the service closed, I made my way back to my parent's pew. My Dad looked serious, but proud as he patted me on my shoulder and said "Praise the Lord, son." I heard the tears in his voice. He was proud of me and I knew it. This was one of the few times in my youth that I felt my Dad's approval. I was grateful for it. Next to him, my Mom stood beaming and dabbing at the corners of her eyes. "We're so happy son. God is so pleased. This is an answer to our prayers." It felt good to have their unabashed approval but it concerned me that what I said and what they thought I said were two different things, but I didn't know how to explain that so I just went along with the celebratory mood.

What I didn't know at that service was that my destiny had been chosen for me. From that night forward, every decision I made would be viewed through the lens of my "surrender to full time Christian service". That phrase meant that I was going to spend my life in some kind of full-time, vocational ministry. God would fill in the details later, since I didn't feel called to preach or be a missionary. Again, I didn't feel *called* to anything. I just knew that I had come to a crossroads in my young life and my pursuit to become godly. Surrendering to God was the next logical step. It was all very manipulative, especially to a young boy, but I thought I was doing the right thing and no one ever questioned me.

That decision meant I could no longer consider a career of my own choosing. It meant I would need to attend a Christian college that would allow me to study for some kind of ministry. It meant I would only date girls who wanted to be the wife of someone in ministry. It meant I would have to give up my selfish desires for God's will, no matter what that meant. It meant I would only work in a church or christian school. It meant I would never strive to make money or make a name for myself. It meant I could only study music in the context of christianity.

The rest of my life was defined by that moment when a pastor cared more about counting the decisions made by people in his church than the people making them. He could now add my name to the tally of decisions made that week during the annual mission's conference. There were several other young people who made similar decisions as well. Mine was perhaps the weakest one, but regardless it looked good because churches and pastors were judged by how many "decisions" were being made regularly in their services. This gave the pastor bragging rights to proclaim how mightily God's Spirit was moving in their congregation. It was one of three evidences of God's blessing on a church. The other two were attendance growth and starting a building campaign to accommodate that growth. At the next fellowship of pastors meeting the conversation would go something like this: "God has really been blessing us and working our midst. At our recent Missions Conference you could really see the Holy Spirit moving amongst us. We had large crowds and people at the altar every night. There were visitors in attendance each night and several got saved. We had young men called to preach and to the mission field. One young lady was called to be a pastor's wife (yes, that was a thing) and one young man surrendered to full-time Christian service! The hand of God was truly on us this week!"

I knew my call to full-time Christian service was at the bottom of the hierarchy of calls from God. It felt a bit like a second class calling. Pastors made it clear that there was no higher calling than that of a young man being called to preach. Some boys were called to be an evangelist, which was a preacher who traveled around and held revival meetings at churches everywhere. Being called to a specific mission field was also a call from God that young men could answer. To be a missionary was held in high esteem since it required great sacrifice. One would move to some exotic land, learn a new language and culture and possibly put their lives at risk while preaching the Gospel to Godless people. Now you may be thinking, "Don't missionaries preach too?" Indeed they do, but for some reason, when you were called to preach you became a "preacher boy" and attained a place of highest favor. Pastors would brag about how many "preacher-boys" they had in their church. There was a special kinship and bond between these preacher-boys and the pastor. Pastors would mentor them and dote on them with the hopes and dreams that some would one day return to their home church and serve on staff there. It was often said that being a preacher was more important than being President of the United States.

*   *   *

It took me until my late 30's before I had the courage to stand up for myself and begin shedding this artificial calling on my life. I now know that this was religious abuse. Whether it was intentional or not, it was abusive. I was manipulated into believing that I had no choice in my life. I could never renege on this decision or I would be going against the calling of God on my life. I would forever be labeled as rebelling against God and that is the last thing I ever wanted to do.

Much to my dismay, my "call" into full-time Christian service did not change my attraction to boys.

There is no greater agony than bearing an untold story in-side you.

— Maya Angelou

PRAYER

"I'm a hopeless mess, God. How am I ever going to get out of this mess I've created? What will I do? Why won't you help me?"

CHAPTER 8
Epiphany

The clock on the office wall read 9pm. It was a cool, autumn, Saturday. I sat alone in my office, my Bible open on my desk along with several study books related to the Sunday School lessons I was preparing for my young adult class the next morning. To my right sat my computer desk cluttered with papers, hymnals and choir music. The screen displayed my half-finished special music and choir schedule for the next month and the order of service for the next morning. I sat staring at my messy, unorganized desk in defeated silence. It was the physical manifestation of my life: chaotically out of control.

The large church building, which would be full of life in the morning, sat empty and unfriendly in the night. The sprawling building was eerily cavernous and unsettling when vacant. My office was halfway down one of two long halls of Sunday school classrooms that extended in opposite directions from the circular structure containing a large half-circle sanctuary, fellowship halls, and additional classrooms. The long, wooden beams in the sanctuary led up to the peak of the circle supporting the steeple on the roof which pointed to God - or at least that's what we hoped.

This was the large independent, fundamental Baptist church in the Peoria, Illinois area where I served as an Assistant Pastor for nine years. It was a bustling place on a Sunday. Up to 500 people would gather each week to sing together, listen to the teaching and preaching, and fellowship with one another. Sunday mornings were full of children and their smiling faces, happily running through the halls to meet their friends waiting in the Sunday School classroom. Music, laughter, and happy chatter seemed to stream from every direction at once. Hugs, handshakes, and warm greetings were given liberally to all who entered the building. The structure itself seemed to be alive and breathing positive energy every Sunday. As people poured into the blue carpeted sanctuary they were welcomed by the pianist and organist playing cheerful, upbeat, evangelistic hymns. It was my church home and the people there were my family. It was my life. I had no friends outside the doors of Bay View Baptist Church.

"There's no place I'd rather be on a Sunday morning!" the pastor would bellow. "You won't find this out in the world. What we have here is something only the Spirit of God can create. This is what people in the world are searching for. It's right here. Say 'Amen' if you're happy to be here today!" It felt good to be a part of something so special and exclusive. I wondered how the rest of the world lived without the peace, love, and joy that only the Holy Spirit could provide. I felt sorry for what they were missing out on. I pondered how miserable they must be living a life so void and meaningless.

I put my heart and soul into creating a good, rousing song service of hymns, select choruses, two choir numbers, an offertory and special music. I crafted the ebb and flow of the worship service which was designed to bring the congregation to just the right place before the pastor took the pulpit to deliver his message from God. I was masterful at creating a dynamic service and people praised me for it. I'm still proud of the music program I built there.

But as I sat alone in my office on that Saturday night, the sounds of laughter and singing were replaced by the creaks and groans of the aging structure. Strange, unidentifiable hums, pops, creeks, and cracks echoed from rooms and hallways far away from my office. The indistinct sound of a door opening and closing in the distance made the hair on my arms stand up when no footsteps followed the sound. I talked myself into believing it was not a door at all, but I never truly believed my own explanation.

The sounds of emptiness often distracted and spooked me. I sat at my desk facing the door which led out into the long, dark hallway barely illuminated by the light from my office and the soft red glow of the exit signs at either end. One end of the hall disappeared into a dark classroom. The other end was a four-way intersection hallway, and all but one extended into darkness curving beyond my sight. The remaining hall led to the well-lit foyer I often used to exit to the parking lot. I didn't like being alone at the church, especially at night.

I sat at my desk staring blankly. Tears welled up in my eyes. *What am I going to do?* I asked myself. *I've ruined everything. I'm going to lose it all as soon as someone finds out. Then what you do, Joel? This is all you know how to do.* I wiped my eyes with the back of my hand. *I can't do this anymore. I can't take it. I have no hope.* This was a recurring conversation I had with myself. Often during the day when the pressure felt more than I could bear, I would wander into the woods behind the church where no one could hear me and there I would sit crying and praying in agony. "God I'm so sorry. Please forgive me. Please help me. I can't do this anymore. I have no strength left. Please help me. Remove this from me. I beg you to change me. Please take this away from me. I'd rather die than live like this. Please just kill me if you won't change me." In the woods I wept and begged until I had nothing left to say. I listened for God and I tried to convince myself that he was listening to me, but I heard nothing. My prayers only clung to the tree branches above me, never seeming to get to God's ears.

I was several years into my successful ministry career as an Assistant Pastor at this thriving Baptist church. The congregation loved and respected me. They praised my work. I was very good at what I did. Yet there I sat, alone in my office, feeling nothing but failure, despair, and hopelessness.

Maya Angelou said, "There is no greater agony than bearing an untold story inside you." This was an agony I was well-acquainted with. I felt completely alone in the universe. No one knew my story and I knew if they did it would change everything in my life. This is why no one must ever know, but how could I possibly keep this secret from being known? Everyone thought of me as a godly man who was living an exemplary life yet in between sermon and Sunday school preparations, I was finding more and more excuses to get out of the office and cruise for sex. I wouldn't admit to myself that I was doing it though. Instead, I played a mental game with myself to reduce the guilt. I would find a legitimate reason to get out of the office; a visit to a church member in the hospital, a stop at the Christian book store to look for a particular resource, or some item I needed to purchase from Sam's Club or Office Depot. I didn't really need an excuse to get out because I was free to come and go, but that excuse allowed me to pretend that I wasn't actually planning on sinning, it just sort of happened along the way to or from my business. Typically I would choose an out-of-the-way route that just *happened* to take me near one of the hot spots that experience had taught me were prime cruising locations. It was a game of chance. Maybe someone would be there or maybe I'd strike out, but the fear of missing out was real so I had to at least do a drive-by. This logic accomplished two tasks:

1. It allowed me to have a legitimate reason to be out of my office.

2. It made me feel less responsible for what happened while I was out which somewhat lessened the guilt that accompanied each of these adventures.

The parks were the easiest to quickly check out. All it took was a couple of drives through while looking for the universal cruising signals: a car parked on the side of the road with a man in the driver's seat who would glance my way and casually nod as I passed him. In that quick glance I had to determine if he was someone of interest to me. If I wasn't sure, another loop around to get a better look or perhaps a flick of his brake lights as I approached from behind. *Drive by slower this time. Yes, he looks attractive and not too old. I'll return the signal.* A quick touch to my own brake lights was all that was required. If he didn't follow me, I would circle back around and repeat the process. It's a complicated, unspoken game of cat and mouse fed by the fear of being caught. It required multiple verifications that the other man wanted the same thing you wanted and wasn't an undercover cop.

What I didn't realize at the time was that most of these other park cruisers were also closeted, married men themselves who shared my fears and concerns. Eventually our two vehicles would end up parked close enough to one another where we could exchange longer glances, a nod, or hand signal. At some point one of us would casually exit his car and pretend to get something out of the trunk, throw some trash away, or kick the tires all while keeping an eye on the guy in the other car. A gentle adjustment of the crotch or a more definite nod was designed to say, "Hey, why don't you join me or follow me?". If there was a wooded trail nearby, one would take the lead and stroll down the trail glancing behind him repeatedly while the other followed at a safe distance until deep into the safer foliage of the trees. If a public restroom was nearby, we'd end up there - always in silence - so we could hear footsteps if anyone were approaching. When the weather was bad, the front seat of the car would suffice. There was little to no conversation, and very little eye contact. We weren't there to make friends. We were there to get off.

If you are doubting any part of what you just read, please know this is not sensational in any way. My description is a window into a major reality of pre-internet gay culture. Closeted gay men had few legitimate outlets for connecting in real life. There is a long, rich history of gay men cruising as I've shared in other places in this book. Men like myself who were gay but married to a woman and presenting as straight found cruising to be the *only* way to find a quick release and a moment of weird intimacy with another man. I thought of it as anything but intimate, but looking back I realize I longed for the intimacy of a man. These quick, anonymous sexual encounters were the only way I could find any semblance of that. I couldn't even imagine what intimacy was. I certainly couldn't fathom experiencing it with a man.

Someone once defined intimacy as "into-me-see". If intimacy is achieved by allowing someone to see inside you - all of you, the good the bad and the ugly - then intimacy was alien to me. I never allowed anyone that level of access to me, not even my wife. I wasn't consciously holding back, but a lifetime of hiding who I was, certain that everyone would reject me, replaced intimacy with performance. I learned how to perform as a good, godly, man, husband, father, and leader. I made sure I checked off all the boxes. After a cruising encounter like I described above, I would atone for my sin by out performing myself. I dove even deeper into being the godly man I was determined to be.

My cruising habit, while providing a brief release from the stress, resulted in even greater stress. The more men I encountered through cruising, the more concerned I was that one of them would walk through the doors of our church on a Sunday morning and recognize me.

I developed a Sunday service ritual which began the moment I walked out on the stage with the choir. I lead them in a rousing opening number and turned to face the congregation and while leading them in an enthusiastic gospel song. I quickly scanned the large fan-shaped auditorium looking for any unfamiliar, yet familiar, faces amongst the hundreds of well-dressed congregants in the pews. I continued to scan the audience until I was certain I was safe. Only after I could put my mind at ease was I able to pour myself unreservedly into the task at hand, knowing that my secret was still safely locked away.

All of this fear was swirling in my mind that Saturday night alone in the church. The growing weight of the shame and guilt I carried everywhere grew especially heavy while the hot tears welled up in my eyes.

It was a new low of hopelessness and impending doom. I recognized my life was inevitably going to come crashing down and there was nothing I could do about it. I sensed it was just a matter of time before the doors and windows of my private world were flung open and everyone would be recoil in horror at what they saw. I knew I would lose everyone and everything. *If only there was someone I could talk to. There must be someone.* But there was no one. I knew that even an admission of being tempted by homosexual feelings would have me ousted from my ministry career. I would never be able to serve again. Ministry was all I knew how to do. I found a book or two about homosexuality at the Christian bookstore, but I was afraid to buy them lest someone see them on my shelf and suspect I bought them for myself. It probably wasn't a rational fear, but I couldn't risk it. No one must suspect Brother Barrett of being gay.

God, what am I going to do?! How am I going to live through this?! Just let me die! Living in constant fear of being discovered normally kept my tears to a minimum, even in the solitude of the woods. But this time, at my desk, the floodgates were opened and I couldn't hold back. The tears spilled down my face. I shook in anguish under the weight of the pain and sadness. I couldn't remember what hope felt like. If I had ever felt hope, I wasn't aware of it. I was utterly hopeless and alone. I had nowhere and no one to turn to for help.

Eyes fixed on my desk, I whispered the words: *I can't keep living like this*. Just then, the movement of someone entering my office caught the corner of my eye. In an instant I jerked up, heart racing, thinking: *Oh great, someone's going to see me crying at my office and know something's wrong! What am I going to tell them?*

Glancing toward the door, I was startled to see no one there. I was still alone, yet I didn't feel alone. Someone ... something had entered my office. I couldn't see it, but I could feel it. It was as if a giant, warm, comforting blanket was suddenly wrapped around me. I felt spooked yet strangely comforted. As the warm presence engulfed me, I heard the reassuring words, "You're going to be okay." There was no audible voice, but inside my heart I heard the message clearly. I didn't know what it meant or where it came from, but I believed it. It felt like truth to me despite any lack of evidence. Something happened that night, a tiny spark of hope flickered in me. It was weak and faint, but it was the first glimmer of hope I remember having in my life. I didn't know how, why, or when I would be okay, but I trusted the message. And then, just as quickly as it appeared in my office, it vanished. And I was once again alone.

In confused, stunned silence I sat, feeling unnerved yet oddly peaceful. *What just happened? Who or what was that?* I will never know. Some would say it was God or an angel. Some would say it was the universe speaking to me. Some might say it was a deeper consciousness. I don't need or want to know. I choose not to define it or seek explanation. What matters to me is that for the first time in my life, I felt hope. I didn't know what it meant to be okay, but I knew I would be. After this peculiar encounter with not only a strange, unseen force but also with myself, I quietly and quickly gathered my things, exited the dark building and went home, wondering what it all meant.

Hello Lord, it's me your child
I have a few things on my mind
Right now I'm faced with big decisions
And I'm wondering if you have a minute, 'cause right now I
don't hear so well
And I was wondering if you could speak up

−Sara Groves, "Hello Lord"

PRAYER

I'm listening God, please, speak to me.

CHAPTER 9
Ex-gay, Still Gay.

Ex-gay therapy, reparative therapy, conversion therapy, pray the gay away, Biblical counseling, or whatever you want to call it - the goal is to help gays eliminate, reduce, or at least manage their unwanted same sex attraction (SSA). These terms are interchangeable and ultimately mean the same thing: You are broken because you are gay. God didn't make you gay, it's you giving into your sinful nature. God doesn't intend for you to sin or live in sin, so there is a way to achieve freedom from this and become among those who claim to be ex-gay.

Today, the term conversion therapy is widely recognized as the umbrella term for all of these techniques. Exodus International used the term ex-gay, so that is what I will use in my story.

While I was in ex-gay therapy I was labeled a "struggler" along with others who were battling with same sex attraction. Even at the time, I wasn't comfortable with being called a struggler. It felt defeating, weak, helpless, and hopeless. Which was the opposite of what I hoped to find in ex-gay therapy. I wondered why they chose such a negative label to place on us, but I didn't question it at first. I was there to get help and hope - even if it meant I had to be labeled a struggler.

People are often surprised to learn that my experience with ex-gay therapy did not include wires, hypnosis, disturbing images, physical or sexual abuse, shock treatment or anything close to that. While many have experienced those horrible things in conversion therapy, my initial sessions were quite typical of any other introductory counseling sessions. As I shared earlier, I told him my life story and he asked things like "And how did that you make you feel?" It was the first time in my life I dared tell anyone the things I told him. It felt good to come clean. We communicated regularly both in person and via email over the next few months. I went to work immediately trying to curb my gay thoughts, desires and behaviors. It wasn't easy but I was determined to "white knuckle" it in hopes that eventually my desires would change or at least diminish considerably. They assured me that the more I practiced new behaviors and thought patterns that I would eventually move from white knuckling it to a more controlled existence of "Casting down imaginations, and every high thing that exalts itself against the knowledge of God, and bringing into captivity every thought to the obedience of Christ." I longed for this kind of self-control. I marveled that according to Exodus, there were many men like myself who had achieved this level of freedom. I was told that they were living happy, heterosexual lives not controlled by homosexual desires. Some were married with children. Some were single and contented to live in celibacy. I wondered how long it would take before I could call myself an ex-gay. Sometimes I fantasized about being one of those national speakers who inspired others with their colorful story of freedom from homosexuality. I imagined my wife and I once again being looked up to as leaders and role models. But that meant she'd have to know my secret. *One step at a time, Joel. Just focus on getting your own help for now.*

The monthly drive from South Bend to Indianapolis to see Brad was three hours one way. After a few months of making the drive he referred me to an Exodus-approved counselor from their nationwide network who was in my area. I was sad to not see Brad anymore, because it meant I'd have to start all over again with a new person. However, I was very happy to have a shorter drive. I wasted no time making the first appointment with Mike Swihart in Elkhart, Indiana. I wanted to keep the momentum going. Mike's office was attached to the side of his home in a residential neighborhood about 25 minutes from me. At this point I was still pastoring my church and had yet to bring my wife into my journey. I was hoping beyond hope that I could quickly and quietly get this all fixed and put behind me once and for all. I hoped my wife and church would never have to know.

Mike - much like my first counselor Brad - also seemed kind, loving and compassionate. He was a short, round man with eyes that squeezed nearly shut when he smiled. An inquisitive expression with a furrowed brow never seemed to leave his face. He listened intently as I poured out my stories, frustrations, and fears week after week. It felt good to again "come clean" with someone who didn't judge me or recoil in horror. Nothing I told him ever seemed to surprise him. I quickly felt at ease with him.

Mike's approach was very different from Brad. It involved more in depth exploration of my upbringing, parents and family, and my adult life as a married man with three children. I cried rivers of tears as we unpacked story after story from my life. I dug deep into my memories hoping to find the key to unlock the mystery of why I was gay. Between visits to his office, he encouraged behavior modification, a change of thought patterns, and lots and lots of prayer. I describe it as pray-the-gay-away. There were some good and healthy things that came out of this counseling. It wasn't all about being gay. In fact, much of it was about the closet inside me where I hid all the feelings about myself, my upbringing, my wife, my religion and my god. I needed to process those feelings. All my life I had willingly accepted the word of the authorities in my life which were primarily the church, my parents, and other religious leaders. I admit, it felt good to give myself permission to grieve the loss of my childhood and the abusive nature of my upbringing. It was liberating to acknowledge how fucked up much of my life really was.

I also worked through the dynamics of my dysfunctional marriage. I was beginning to realize how severely broken our relationship was. I had never been in any kind of counseling before, so I relished the opportunity to have someone analyze my life.

However, at the root of the counseling was an effort to help me discover why I had sexualized men and formed these unhealthy thought and behavior patterns. If we could figure that out, then we could begin changing the way I thought and start rerouting the ruts in my brain and form new, healthier ones. Mike described it as sexual healing and transformation.

Most of the foundation of the ex-gay movement was built upon early, non-scientific ideas that homosexuality was caused by some external force because no one was born gay. In order to become ex-gay, I needed to sort through every relationship, trauma, teaching, and attitude that could be the root cause of me being gay.

Every ex-gay book I read, every speaker I listened to, and both counselors all began with this line of questioning:

"What was your relationship like with your dad? Was he emotionally or physically absent? Was he abusive?"

"Tell me about your mother. Was she overbearing and dominant? Were you extremely close to her?"

"Tell me about your sexual history. Was there any sexual abuse? When did you first experiment sexually and with who?"

"How did you develop sexually? Do you masturbate? Do you fantasize about men? What sexual thoughts and fantasies have gone unchecked?"

The ex-gay movement was born from the church and remains connected to religion. It is built up on the foundation that homosexuality is unnatural and a sin against God, or at least "acting out" on your homosexual desires is a sin.

I was taught the Bible says that even thinking about a sinful act was the same as committing it. This made me doubt if I could ever make all that work. It seemed to me that God's plan was an all-or-nothing arrangement that I could never live up to. When I inquired about this, I was told not to focus on that and to just take it one day at a time, with a focus on trying to do the most right and the least wrong each day. This seemed like permission to sin to me, but I went along with it anyway. I was encouraged to look at it like a spectrum of "acting out". One extreme of the spectrum was hooking up and having sex. The other extreme was something like thinking a brief, lustful thought. Somewhere in the middle were things like looking at porn or masturbating. The more I pondered this the more confused I became. I was taught all my life that God makes no distinction between sins. "Sin is sin!" the preachers would say. "All have sinned and come short of the Glory of God! It makes no difference how big or how small the sin. God hates sin. Sin separates you from God." So in addition to God's all-or-nothing plan, there was an accompanying damned-if-you-do, damned-if-you-don't arrangement. But I wanted to please God, be straight, save my marriage, and stay in ministry so I kept on trying to make this make sense in my mind. It never did.

Over the weeks, months, and ultimately years, I sat in the counselor's office for umpteen hours talking and talking. I kept hoping to land upon the reason I was gay. I considered my parents and the weird evolution from fairly normal people to extreme fundamentalist Baptist. My family was always considered too extreme by even the other people in the conservative churches we attended. My parents were viewed as confrontational troublemakers in the church because they were always displeased with something. Thus, we hopped from church to church most of my life. I pondered my dad, a stern, sober man who was prone to angry outbursts. He had little in common with me. Our relationship was always distant and awkward. While I knew he loved me, I never felt emotionally connected to him ... *maybe that's why I'm gay?*

Or maybe it was because my mother and I were very close when I was young? She and I had so much in common. We loved music, nature, art, creating things together, cooking and more. I did feel a deep connection to her. She sometimes affectionately called me Jewell and reminded me of how special I was. During some particularly rough financial times of life when my Dad was unemployed and we were living in poverty, she inappropriately confided in me about her frustrations with my Dad. As I matured, I grew to resent her. I realized she was quite passive aggressive and difficult to please. Sometimes I even felt sorry for my Dad. *Maybe she's the reason I'm gay?*

I considered the horrible, isolated teen years I endured when I had no friends or social outlets. Those years were filled with many dark and lonely times where fantasy and masturbation became my best friend. *Maybe that's why I'm gay?*

I really, really wanted to find the reason I am gay. I dug deep into my memories hoping to unlock the secret. Looking back, I'm not sure what good I thought that knowledge would do but it seemed like the first step to fixing me. In session after session with the counselor, I pulled out painful memories of my parents, the church, school, and foggy recollections of other events in the hopes it would provide the missing piece of the puzzle to solve the mystery. I wanted something to blame. It would relieve me of the responsibility.

Sexual abuse. That's it! If I were sexually abused it would make sense why I am gay because from what I've been told, most gay men are that way because of the sexual abuse in their background. I had never told anyone about John before, but I decided it was time.

"When I was about twelve or thirteen there was this boy named John, who was always trying to get in my pants every time he came over." Shame engulfed my being as I shared this dark secret long hidden inside me.

"I hated it and yet I loved it. I longed for him to come over, but I felt so guilty after he left." I dabbed at my eyes with a tissue from the box nearby. The counselor, a plump man in his forties, with his brow creased in deep furrows, leaned forward in his chair as if he were thinking "Ah, now we're getting somewhere." He looked deep into my eyes. "How do you feel about that now, Joel?"

"I don't know. I am confused by it all. Was I abused? Is that sexual abuse? Is that why I'm gay? Is it my fault? I don't know. I did want it and enjoyed it, but I also felt awful about it. Sometimes I told him we weren't going to do that anymore, but the next time he came over we did it again. I liked it and he did too. I'm so confused, I don't know what I feel about it." My voice was high and shaking and my face was hot and wet with tears.

The counselor sat intently staring at me in silence for what felt like much too long. It felt like he was trying to look into the depths of my soul. The longer he stared, the more uncomfortable and emotional I became. Crossing my arms, I held myself and rocked back and forth while really wanting to just curl up on the sofa in a fetal position. "Why am I this way?! I can't take this." Finally, in a hushed, calm and quiet voice he said "Joel, let's pray."

I closed my swollen eyes and slumped back in the small, floral-print sofa and listened. "Lord, Father, you see how much pain my brother Joel is in today. I'm asking that you show him your love. Wrap your arms around him and hold him. I'm asking that you reveal to him what you want him to know about this part of his life. Speak to him. Reveal yourself to him in his pain." He fell silent again for a moment and then in a voice barely above a whisper, he said, "Joel, listen to what the Holy Spirit is saying to you. God wants you to know something. What is He saying to you? What is on your heart?"

I sat in the awkward silence, choking back tears while desperately trying to listen and search my heart and mind for some message from God. I spent my ministry career preaching and teaching people that God is speaking to us about anything and everything if we just listen with our hearts to the still, small voice of God. Clutching the wadded up tissue in my hand, I waited and listened and searched, hoping to hear something…anything. I heard nothing. After a prolonged silence, with a faltering voice I said "I…I…I don't hear anything. I don't know what God is saying to me." With eyes still tightly shut, Mike began praying again. "Father, you know Joel's heart. I'm asking that you make yourself known to him in this moment and speak to his heart."

"Joel, listen to what God is saying to you." He fell silent again.

As I sat in the silence searching my mind for some message from God, I became aware of the ticking of the clock on the wall behind me. In the quiet of the room the clock seemed to get louder. Tick-tock, Tick-Tock, TICK-TOCK, TICK!-TOCK! I tried to ignore it but it only amplified in the silence of the tiny office. A muffled voice announced, "You're listening to WFRN" from the radio in the equally small waiting room on the other side of the thin wall behind me. The muffled music seeped through the wall. My mind became divided between trying to listen to God and playing name that tune with each Christian contemporary song that came on. I recognized the familiar intro to a favorite Newsboys song and began singing along in my mind...*Joel! Stop! Stop getting distracted! Listen to God!* I mentally reprimanded myself. In my struggle to refocus on listening to God, Mike's voice broke my stream of consciousness. "Joel, what is God saying to you right now? What is on your heart?"

"I don't know." I sighed disappointedly, "I'm trying, I really am, but I don't hear anything except the clock ticking behind me and the music in the other room..." before I could say more he interrupted in a startlingly loud and authoritative voice. "Spirit of confusion, you leave Joel alone. In the name of Jesus, we bind you and remind you that you have no authority over my brother here. Satan, I bind you and your spirits of confusion from distracting Joel." in a softer voice he continued, "Father God, Jesus, you see my brother Joel here struggling. Satan has sent his demons to confuse and distract him. We're asking you in the name of Jesus and his precious blood to bind those spirits and reveal yourself to Joel right now. He's confused and hurt and wants to hear from you." A little frightened, I hugged myself closer and sunk deeper into the sofa. "Now Joel, listen to God's voice in you. What is He saying to you? What does God want you to know."

Again, in silence, I searched my heart and mind for some secret message from God but found only frustration accompanied by the ticking clock and the muffled radio. I wondered why I only heard silence. God knew I wanted nothing more than to hear some divine, life-changing, message that would help me understand why I am gay. What is this cruel game he was playing with me?

I'm finally here in complete surrender getting the help I need and where is God? Has he given me over to a reprobate mind and forsaken me? Have I tested his patience beyond his mercy and now I've committed the unpardonable sin? Why is he silent?!

My mind raced and bounced from thought to thought, question to question. "Joel, what are you feeling? God sees your tears. What is he saying to you? Why the tears?" he asked. "I don't know. I just feel so overwhelmed by all of this. I don't know what God is saying and I don't even know why I'm crying."

"You're in pain Joel. That's pain. Let God speak to you through your tears." Then he began praying again.

"God, my brother Joel is hurting so much. He is in pain. He is confused. I'm asking that you reveal yourself to Joel in this moment."

He was right about one thing: I was in pain. I was peeling back the layers of thirty plus years of life and feeling the pain of being honest with myself and others for the first time in my life. It was three decades of my life that I had denied. It was the pain of my youth when I felt completely alone and uncared for. It was the pain of trying to please a God that now refused to even whisper to me. It was the pain of a co-dependent relationship with my wife. It was the pain of hiding who I was. It was the pain of the church mocking and shaming me.

There were no words for this kind of pain. I squinted through my nearly closed eyes. He sat a few feet in front of me, eyes tightly closed and leaning slightly forward with a concerned frown on his face. I shut my eyes and attempted to once again concentrate on the mysterious voice of God that I wasn't hearing. The hiss and whine of the school bus stopping outside reminded me of the time of day. I wondered if our session was nearly over. I wanted to look at the clock ticking behind me, but that would have required me turning around in my seat. The voices of children drifted in from the street outside. I thought of my own children. *What if they find out? What if I have to tell them? How are they ever going to survive all of this? I've failed as a parent. They must never know.* A door slammed from inside the counselor's house. I could hear the muffled sounds of his children talking about their day.

"Joel." his soft voice jerked my mind back to reality. I opened my eyes. He looked serious and alarmingly concerned. "Joel, Satan is trying to keep you from hearing God's voice, but Satan has no control over you because you are a child of God. You are not Satan's. So I want you to continue to focus on God's voice each day between now and our next session. Ask God to speak to you and listen for his voice." His face relaxed into a gentle smile as he sat back in his overstuffed chair. In an instant, the atmosphere changed and he casually grabbed his scheduling book. "Now how is two weeks from today?"

That's it? We're done? I felt frustrated that I had yet another appointment in a long string of appointments where I wasn't sure what we had accomplished. *What am I supposed to do with all of that now?* I pushed my negative thoughts aside and booked another appointment two weeks out.

In addition to individual appointments I also attended a group therapy meeting with four or five other guys like myself in his small office. I was tempted to hook up with one or two of them, but I never did. We crowded into the office, sitting elbow-to-elbow and shared our sexual struggles and colorful histories. I wasn't sure of the purpose of the meeting, but it felt good to know I wasn't alone ... so I attended. Sometimes we cried, sometimes we laughed as we shared the struggles we faced since our last time together. I think we each held back the ugliest part of ourselves, but we shared fairly openly about our masturbation habits, viewing porn, facing temptations, or meeting up with other men since our last session. On at least one occasion, the Methodist pastor Kevin appeared in the group at my invitation. I thought it might help him even though it wasn't really helping me. The minister in me wanted to help others. He and I did hook up again at least one more time before going our separate ways.

I spent countless hours in individual and group therapy. I went to a weekend retreat at a lodge in the hills of Pennsylvania. All the men in attendance were seeking help with issues related to sex. I questioned the wisdom of having us all sleeping in the same house when most of us were attracted to one another. I was disappointed that nothing sexual happened with the handsome, sandy-haired guy I met there. I went to conferences, read every book recommended to me, listened to the national speakers and watched their videos, opened up to a few people in my life and achieved new levels of authenticity. I modified my behavior with little success. I did everything I could to not be gay.

I spent nearly three years repeating all parts of the manipulative and disappointing process. I had short seasons of what might be called "success" where I wasn't acting out as often, but there was never a moment where I was free of my attractions, homosexual thoughts, or desire to connect with men whether in a chat room or out cruising. On numerous occasions, I came across men from the group or from the large evangelical church I was attending in a cruisy bathroom or sketchy situations. It caused me to wonder if anyone was really experiencing the freedom from homosexuality that was promoted to me. I, for sure, was not. If I had to describe it on a scale of 1-10 with one being where I was when I started and ten being completely set free, after nearly 3 years I was at a 1.2 at best. I was growing very weary of trying to find the freedom and transformation that the ex-gay leaders proclaimed. If God wanted me to not be gay, and I was pouring my heart and soul into the journey, he wasn't even meeting me half-way. I began to question how much more of this I could endure. Something had to give.

I can see clearly now the rain is gone.
I can see all obstacles in my way.
Here is that rainbow I've been praying for.
It's gonna be a bright
Bright sunshiny day.

—Johnny Nash, "I Can See Clearly Now"

PRAYER

"God, could it be that you love and accept me just the way I am?"

CHAPTER 10
The UnEXpected Gift

"Joel, you've never allowed anyone to get close enough to know you. You've pre-judged everyone. You've determined in advance that you must never let anyone close enough to know you or they will reject you. You don't actually know if people love you as you are because no one knows who you are." Brad - my counselor through Exodus International - had a point.

"But I know how people feel about homosexuality. I've heard it all my life. If anyone found out I had these feelings they would reject me. I've seen them mock men like me from the pulpit. I've heard my mother's fear and disgust. I've heard the words dripping with venomous hate. I know what people think." I reasoned with him.

"I understand what you're saying Joel, but I want to encourage you to consider that perhaps you've become judgmental of the judgmental and intolerant of the intolerant. It isn't fair to you or them. Again, you're pre-judging people and taking away their opportunity to know you and choose to love you or reject you. You've already determined they will reject and hate you, but the truth is you don't actually know what they are thinking or how they will respond."

I sat in silence considering this new perspective. He was right. I was surprised that the counselor didn't defend the church and environment I was in. But even to right-leaning evangelicals, the independent, fundamental Baptists were often considered extreme, legalistic, and problematic. By this time in my life, I too was beginning to reject that brand of Christianity, but the damage of thirty-six years was deep and traumatic. I was thankful for someone to acknowledge with me that the churches and belief system of my life wasn't healthy or balanced. It was intolerant, judgmental, and yes … abusive.

It was understandable how fearful I was of letting anyone see the real me. It frightened me to my core. I was already losing any meaningful relationship with my parents even when they weren't fully aware of what was going on in my life. I soon discovered the truth about the relationship with my sister, the one person in my family with whom I felt the closest. When I called to share I was going through ex-gay therapy to get the help I needed for the homosexual desires I had, she listened in silence and then said, "Well I guess I'll have to love the love the sinner but hate the sin." She ended our relationship after that conversation by never speaking to me again or offering any form of support, encouragement or understanding. And that hasn't changed.

Later in my journey I came out to my mom who sat staring in horror at me as if I had suddenly turned red and grown horns. All she could utter was, "What did we do wrong?" She and my dad cut their visit short and drove the four hours back home that night instead of staying to spend time with their grandchildren. My mother never came to terms with it all and rarely spoke to me after that. She sent letters full of condemning scripture, religious pamphlets and her words of warning. One of the first letters I received from her after that night contained the line: "I can't believe my son is a Sodomite." After quitting ex-gay therapy, my oldest brother cut me out of his life too. He told me he never wanted to see my "gay lover" again. My remaining brother and his wife chose to cut me off when I made it clear that I didn't want their constant tears and pleas for me to come back to God. My family has caused tremendous pain in my life. They have said and done hateful and horrible things to me and my husband that are unacceptable and ungodly by any standard. I went through some very difficult weeks and months before I realized I don't need people like this in my life regardless of our blood relation. While it took some effort and therapy, I was able to let go of my expectations around who I thought they should be and instead find a place of healing, peace, and strength. I no longer feel any pain related to my siblings or now deceased parents.

When someone shows you who they are, believe them the first time. - Maya Angelou

Like the ex-gay therapist said, "Joel, which is better? You can assume people love you but wouldn't if they knew the truth or you can let them see the truth and give them the opportunity to love you as you are or walk away? Wouldn't it be better to KNOW someone loves you than to assume their love isn't real?" He was right. It is much better to know than to live in fear or ignorance. This is not an attempt to make my family look bad or seek some sort of revenge. I share these experiences to illustrate how the fear I held about others was justified based on their responses and behaviors.

For most of my life I assumed everyone only loved who they thought I was. I had no idea if anyone in the world actually loved me unconditionally. *Would anyone love me if they knew the truth? Do I really want those people in my life if they only love me because they don't know me?*

"Joel, you've also never had authentic relationships with men. You've always sexualized men and made them the object of your lust."

This wasn't entirely true, but there was a grain of truth in it. Just like a young heterosexual man spends much of his life thinking about sex with women, I did spend much of my life fantasizing about sex with men. I did long for the physical touch of a man. I did desire the men I was attracted to, but I did not sexualize all men. However, it is a man's world and I never felt like I really fit in or could relate to it. I always felt like I was on the outside looking in and longing to be one of the boys. I wasn't good at anything that men were supposed to be good at. I didn't like the same things men were supposed to like. I wasn't competitive. Men intimidated me. I felt like a misfit; an outsider.

"I'd like you to carefully choose a couple of men in your life to open up to and tell them what is going on in your world. It will give you a chance to experience what it is like to be real with a man and bond over something non-sexual." The thought of doing this terrified me. I could already feel the rejection.

One of the commitments I made to myself when I began ex-gay therapy was to give it my all and do whatever the counselors said, no matter how crazy or scary sounded. I knew this was my last chance to fix myself, there was nothing more to do after ex-gay therapy. *Don't blow it, Joel!* I reminded myself.

On the three-hour drive back to South Bend I began pondering every man I knew. *Who can I trust? How do I know I can trust them? What if I'm wrong? What if this backfires on me? What if they tell everyone my secret?* I don't recall who I first confided in, but I remember talking to my friend Dan who was a pastor's son and very involved in his church as a leader. We met at a small coffee shop. With a trembling voice, I told him something like, "Dan, I need to tell you something about me. I've been seeing a counselor because I've struggled all my life with homosexuality."

Dan was a very handsome, muscular, blond-haired guy several years younger than me. I was very attracted to him, but I never dared reveal that to him. To my surprise, without hesitation he responded compassionately, "Oh wow, Joel. I had no idea. I hope you know we love you anyway. What can I do to help?" I was shocked and relieved. I allowed Dan to see the real me and he didn't reject me. This was the first crack in the mask I had worn all my life.

Later after coming out to my wife and resigning from my church, my family and I moved to nearby Elkhart and began attending a large, community church with contemporary worship services that felt refreshingly casual and comfortable after my years in fundamentalist churches. In this new environment, it was not uncommon for a secular song or movie clip to accompany the pastor's message. That would never have been acceptable in the churches I was a part of.

I tried opening up to a few more men in my life, and most of them were connected to our new church. This felt like the perfect place for me and my family to invisibly blend in while still finding spiritual food and a community without any strings attached. It felt like a progressive and welcoming place, but that was only because they didn't know the real me.

I began singing in the choir and even subbed for the choir director at times. I confided in one of the pastors on staff there because I thought he was someone who might relate to my journey and be supportive of me. He seemed compassionate when I opened up to him. He offered kind words and a listening ear which made me feel at ease with this new friend. It was about two weeks later when I walked into the church on a Sunday morning and was pulled aside by him into a small room where I was surrounded by several men who introduced themselves as elders of the church. I barely knew one or two of them; the rest were strangers to me. To my surprise, they knew all about me - including my secret. They expressed their grave concern for me and my homosexuality. They offered their undefined "support" which I neither needed nor wanted. I was left feeling angry and hurt. My confidence had been broken and now complete strangers were pretending to care about me.

Shortly afterwards, I was ushered into the head pastor's office. He also expressed very serious concern for me. "You do agree that homosexuality is a sin, right?" he asked. "You understand that until you are free of this, it limits how you can serve in River Oaks Community Church? You are welcome to attend here while you get help, but you will not be able to serve in any leadership role." I felt ambushed and targeted. Word spread quickly among those who knew us. It didn't take long for me to feel the distance others were keeping from me. I saw the side glances and conversations and soon decided to quit attending the church. I could never look at it the same way. Churches often use the phrase, "Everyone's welcome!" in their marketing and signage but everyone knows when they aren't welcome. I was no longer welcome.

Why am I sharing all these stories of rejection? They are part of my story, but they aren't the entire story. There was another pastor on staff at that church who befriended me. He wasn't like the others. He didn't seem to care whether I was gay or not - he just appreciated me as a person. Our friendship blossomed even after I left the church. He eventually left vocational ministry and remained friends with me.

The feeling of having a few people love me just as I was outweighed the rejection and judgement of those who did not. The joy of being authentically me was now springing up in my heart and couldn't be squelched. I could see the value in knowing who loved me unconditionally and who did not. I began to view those who showed their ugliness as a gift that allowed me to let them go. This only fueled my growing commitment to transparency and authenticity. While my relationships were smaller in quantity they were much stronger in quality. However, the list was growing in number and in strength.

As the list grew, so did my confidence in who I was. I quit trying to look, act, and speak the part of a straight man and allowed self-expression in ways that I had always repressed. I had spent my life trying to hide the gay in order for people to accept me. And yet now, as I began embracing all the sides of me, to my astonishment, people seemed to like me even more! I wasn't REbuilding life, I was building life for the very first time and I liked who I saw! I had men in my life who loved me as I was and I didn't sexualize them. I had a best friend from college, Gloria, who was with me every step of the way. I had coworkers at the coffee shop I managed who were friends and thought nothing of me being gay. It seemed the more authentically I lived and the less I hid, the more people were attracted to me. I felt like Sally Field saying, "You like me! You really like me!"

It gradually dawned on me that the ex-gay counselor was right about one thing: it felt good to be loved for who I was. However, the joke was on him. It didn't take away my gay. Instead, it taught me that I really could be myself just the way I am and there was a world of people out there who would love me unconditionally. Why would I want to be around people who said they cared about me, but only loved me as long as I was who they thought I should be? I don't need that in my life. Why am I trying so hard to change something that doesn't matter to anyone except the people who only love me conditionally? Thank you ex-gay therapy, for unintentionally helping me accept myself as an OUT GAY MAN. You thought I needed to be set free and you were right...but you had it all wrong. I didn't need to change who I was, I needed to accept who I was. That is true freedom.

PRAYER

"God, if you have a problem with me, you just let me know. You do whatever you need to get my attention. I'll be listening."

CHAPTER 11
Coming Out To Me and God

"Brad, I'm discouraged. I don't feel like I'm making any real progress." I typed the words in an email to the director of the state of Indiana for Exodus International. I wasn't seeing Brad any more, but I did stay in touch with him via email where I occasionally shared my ups and downs and sought encouragement while continuing my ex-gay counseling with Mike.

"It's been almost three years, Brad. I'm doing everything asked of me. I've given my all to this. While some days are slightly better than others, every day is a constant, consuming struggle. I need to know it's going to get better than this."

The internal conversation I was having was more direct: *If this is as good as it gets, I don't want it. I can't live like this. I don't want to live thinking about myself and my sexual desires nearly every moment of the day.*

I analyzed each day to determine to what degree it was a success or a failure. I wasn't sure what success looked like. No one could ever quite define that for me, but I certainly knew that everything felt like failure. *This is no way to live.* I told myself. *I miss the days when I just... lived.*

Ironically, being in ex-gay therapy forced me to think more about sex, sexual attractions, and sexual behaviors than ever before in life. In an effort to "take captive every thought" as the Bible put it, I thought about every thought. I analyzed every behavior. "Change your habits." the counselor advised. "Don't drive by the places that are tempting to you. Don't go places where you might be tempted." Seriously? I was tempted by any place there were men. I couldn't walk through the shopping mall with my wife and children without eyeing every man who passed and being eyed back by many of them. My gaydar was highly tuned. I could tell in a split second if there was interest or curiosity from other men. Changing my driving route to avoid the parks I knew were "cruisy" only took me to new places that might also be "cruisy". It was a hopeless cause. Men were my forbidden fruit and men were everywhere. There was no avoiding them. I was trapped in a maze of men and at my wit's end.

"Brad, can you please connect me to some normal guys like myself who are farther down the road on this journey than me? I've heard the national speakers, but I'd really like to connect with real guys like me who might be willing to be an encouragement and say, 'Hey Joel, just hang in there. I remember when I was where you are. Trust me, it gets so much better.' I don't know anyone like this. All the guys I'm in group therapy with aren't any farther along in this journey than I am. We're all in the same exact place, wallowing in frustration and struggle." Since Brad was the state director for Exodus International, I was certain he must have access to a large database of success stories from men who would be happy to be an encouragement to other men on their journey. I was wrong.

At this point in my journey I felt like the poster boy of ex-gay therapy. For nearly three years I sat in individual counseling several times a month. Once a month I sat in group therapy with several other men who "suffered" from some sort of sexual "brokenness". I read books like *Desires In Conflict*, *Wild At Heart* and other recommended readings. I went to the ex-gay conferences and workshops. I modified my behaviors. I continued to read my Bible, pray, and build non-sexual relationships with men in my life. I was committed to living authentically. I became more and more transparent about who I was and what I was dealing with. Yet despite all of it, nothing was changing in me.

Is this as good as it gets? If so, I don't want it.

I was excited to see Brad's email response pop up on my screen. I quickly printed out the email without reading it and left to go pick up my kids after school from my soon-to-be ex-wife's home. The school bus had not yet arrived so I parked my car in the driveway, took a seat in the grassy yard, and excitedly unfolded the email in anticipation of fresh words of encouragement and motivation. *Brad understands and is connected to Exodus International. I'm sure he's sent me a handful of men I could contact.* I unfolded the paper and saw a short email message that changed my life. It read something like this:

"Joel, each struggler's journey is unique. It is not linear. The degree of "freedom" varies greatly from person to person. I can't tell you when or if you'll experience that freedom or what it will look like. Some men experience complete freedom from homosexuality and go on to live normal, healthy, heterosexual lives with wives and children. Other men struggle their entire life to diminish their homosexual desires, but never find complete freedom. They remain committed to Christ and not acting out on their desires. I am unable to connect you with any other men because nearly all of the men I work with fall into one of two categories:

1) This was a secret part of their life that no one knew about. They are ashamed of it, and want no one to know about it. They came to Exodus, got the help they needed and moved on. It is a closed chapter of their life that they don't talk about with anyone.

2) This was a part of their life. They came to Exodus, got help and moved on ... but they are afraid if they were to talk to someone like you, they would just fall back into it.

I sat in the sunlight of the yard stunned at his words. I read and reread them, especially the part about the two kinds of "successes". Exodus was an international organization with 250 ministries in the USA and 169 ministries in 17 other countries. *You're telling me that the typical "freedom" for a struggler is to live in shame or fear? These are my options?! Shame? Fear? I've spent my entire life living with these two unwanted companions and now after nearly three years of this, you tell me that you don't have ONE success story that is willing to talk me? And now I find out that I have come full circle to once again living in shame or fear? So this really is as good as it gets?!* Something clicked inside me that day.

I stood up, crumpled the email into a ball and threw it on the ground. With unprecedented resolve and disregard for who might hear me, I said aloud, "Then I'm done. I have a life to live and I won't live it like this."

With those words, I gave myself the permission I didn't know I needed. Permission to stop trying to not be gay. Permission to be me. The problem was, I didn't know how to be that version of me. I felt a courageous resolve, yet fear and doubt immediately crept in and whispered: "That's easier said than done, Joel. What will people think? How will you live? What about your children? You're too old to start over again. What does it even mean to be gay? How do you think you're going to do this? Where do you think you're going? How are you going to live?"

These were valid questions. I sat back down in the grass and pondered them. I didn't know the answers. They were all forward facing questions. I couldn't predict the future. *I don't know what's ahead of me, I only know what's behind me.* In a moment of some of the greatest clarity I've ever experienced, I had this mental picture of myself:

I stood on a winding trail at the top of a high hill looking forward. The trail wandered down in front of me and disappeared deep into a dark, foreboding forest where I lost sight of it. Not knowing where it led was more than a little unsettling. I tried to imagine it but couldn't wrap my head around a reality that was so foreign to me. Fear of the unknown and all the maladies awaiting me began creeping up inside. *You could always go back, Joel.* I turned around on the trail and faced the path behind me that led back to all the very familiar places and people in my life. I could see clearly where that trail led and I knew it well. It was familiar, I knew exactly how to walk that path. There is comfort in familiarity. I knew how to be all that everyone on that path expected me to be. But I could also feel the heaviness of the burden returning and the suffocating feeling of who I would have to be if I turned back and retraced my steps. I recalled the lyrics to a Christian song by Sara Groves, a favorite artist at that time in my life:

> *The future feels so hard*
> *And I want to go back*
> *But the places they used to fit me*
> *Cannot hold the things I've learned*
> *Those roads were closed off to me*
> *While my back was turned*
> *The past is so tangible*
> *I know it by heart*
> *Familiar things are never easy*

To discard
I was dying for some freedom
But now I hesitate to go
I am caught between the Promise
And the things I know

Despite the fear of what might lie ahead, I was now certain that going back was no longer an option. I turned back to face the winding trail to the unknown and said to myself: *I don't know where this trail leads, but I know where the one behind me leads and I won't go back to that. I'd rather move forward into the unknown than go back. I'm not going back, ever.*

It felt like I just dove into the deep end of the pool after spending years dipping my toes into the water to test the temperature. I was truly scared, but I was ready to sink or swim. I was coming out to me but I knew I also needed to come out to God. So with a deep breath, I put aside the fear of his judgement and the promised trials and tribulations that would befall me for not following his will and had this conversation with him:

God, if you are who I was taught you are, then you know everything. Which means you know me better than I even know myself. You see me as I am, inside and out. You love me. You lead me. You can speak to me. So you also know how hard I've tried for the last 35 years to not be this way and you also know it's not working. You know that I've given it my all. You've seen my heart.

I'm just letting you know that as of today I am going to live as gay man. I don't even know what that means, but I do know I'm not going to live this way anymore. I don't know what the future holds, but I do know what the past looks like and I'm done. I'm not going back to that.

Now God, I was always taught that you want your children to do right and will lead, guide, and convict them if they aren't doing the right thing or aren't making the right decisions. So I'm asking you to let me know if you have a problem with me. Please do whatever you have to do to get my attention. I promise, I will be listening.

There's a story in the Old Testament about a disgruntled prophet led by God to a wilderness place where he would wait to hear God speak to him. The prophet sat inside the entrance to a cave and waited. As the prophet waited in anticipation, God sent a mighty wind so strong that it broke rocks into pieces. Much to the prophet's dismay, God said nothing. Then, God sent a terrifying earthquake that shook the ground. When it stopped, the prophet again heard nothing. Next, God sent a great fire, but after it was extinguished, the befuddled prophet still heard nothing at all. Perplexed by God's behavior, he asked why he wasn't speaking to him through these powerful forces. God quietly led him deeper into the cave and left him there in the silence. As the prophet stood in the silence of nothingness, he slowly realized that God's voice was the silence.

It has been many years since that day in the grassy yard on a busy street where I came out to me and came out to God. I now know God said everything when he said nothing at all.

PRAYER

Shouted to the Universe: "Happy Pride!"

CHAPTER 12
My First Pride

"Happy Pride!" the stranger leaning out the second-floor window shouted to us as he raised his mimosa in a toast. The large rainbow flag hanging vertically from the window sill softly rippled in the gentle, morning breeze. "Happy Pride!" We shouted back with a wave as we walked past on the sidewalk below.

"Happy Pride!" the smiling lesbian couple walking arm in arm greeted us as they passed us on the sidewalk.

"Happy Pride, boys!" came the greeting from a large, open porch where several young men in rainbow clothing sat raising their cocktails in the air in a toast to us.

"Woo hoo! Happy Pride!" came the shout over the loud thudding music from inside the brownstone full of laughter and happy voices. Rainbow swag and flags adorned the majority of porches and windows we passed. As we neared the intersection of Roscoe and Halsted, the sounds of the lively crowd gathering for the parade grew louder with every step. Our friends Carlos and Ricky lived steps away from the parade route. Their apartment would be our home base for the day. I quickened my pace in anticipation of all I was about to experience at my first Gay Pride parade and all the festivities associated with it.

When people ask me when I came out, I jokingly answer, "I didn't come out ... I oozed out" because coming into my own as a gay man took time. There I was in my late thirties and finally finding the freedom to attend the Chicago Gay Pride that I had heard so much about. David and I were less than a year into our relationship when he invited me to attend with him. Without hesitation, I accepted. Gay Chicago wasn't foreign to me, but Pride was. Even before I met David it wasn't uncommon for me to drive over to Chicago and soak up what was then known as BoysTown. It felt almost utopian. Rainbows were everywhere. Gay bars, underwear shops, vintage thrift stores, stylish men's clothing stores, bathhouses, sex toy shops, and gay owned restaurants lined the street. Gay couples freely walked arm in arm up and down the sidewalks. No one blinked an eye or gave a second look to even the most outlandishly, gender-bending person on the street. It was the most free place I had ever been in my sheltered life and now I was there for one of the largest Pride celebrations in the nation.

Up until this point, all I knew about gay pride was what I heard from the pulpit. I was anxious to see if it lived up to the hedonistic, pearl-clutching, overtly sexual images described to me. I wasn't sure what to expect, but I was excited and ready to experience whatever came my way.

We arrived at Ricky and Carlos' building with four gallons of homemade sangria to add to the day-long festivities at their apartment. With us was a friend of David's who we picked up on our way into the city. She was only the second trans woman I had knowingly met at the time. She was a stunning Puerto Rican woman named Ava. I was enthralled by her story, her beauty, and her vivacious personality. She had an infectious, hearty laugh that filled my heart with joy because it was so obvious how happy she was to be living her authentic self - openly and unashamedly.

As the three of us ascended the flight of stairs to the third floor apartment, we could hear the music of Madonna spilling down the stairs from above us. The thudding beat grew louder and louder as we climbed each stair. On each landing we could also hear the sounds of joyful laughter, dance music, and loud conversations from inside each apartment. It seemed the whole world was celebrating. My heart was already filled with happiness at all I was absorbing and I wasn't even inside our destination yet.

Once at their door we found it ajar and walked into the sunny apartment to find it filled with bright, festive rainbow decor, tables loaded with Ricky's finest culinary creations, and a well-stocked bar of endless possibilities. Our hosts opened their arms wide and embraced me with love and acceptance. I was instantly a part of their chosen family. Scattered throughout the apartment were groups of people from all walks of life, genders, identities, chatting with food and drink in their hands. Like any good gathering of people, we quickly and easily got acquainted. Rotating around the apartment, talking and sharing tidbits about our lives, children, homes, jobs, and all the rest. If a particularly iconic song came on the playlist, a spontaneous dance party might break out. The "classics" were new to me, but I quickly learned to appreciate these infectious dance songs. I hid my ignorance for fear of being judged for not knowing the music of my generation and people. I was surprised that more than a few of those present were straight. Some even brought their children. I'm still connected to many of the people I met that day.

Around mid-morning, the noise of the crowd down the block was getting noticeably louder. Police sirens could be heard in the distance which signaled the approaching parade would soon begin passing by. We readied our cocktails to go, applied sunscreen, and began the short walk up the block to find a place on the parade route. The streets were filled with sounds of celebration from every direction. Happy voices, loud music, shouts of laughter drifted from nearly every building, window, porch, or patio. Rainbow flags were everywhere. Everyone we encountered smiled and greeted us with "Happy Pride!" I had never been around so many gay, gay-friendly, or LGBTQ people in my life. I saw people that looked like me and people that definitely looked nothing like me. Old, young, black, brown, white, male, female, trans, cis, gay, straight - they were all there and celebrating.

The Chicago Pride parade stretches on for miles and lasts several hours from beginning to end. It draws over one million, exuberant, people who crowd the streets and sidewalks to wildly cheer on the colorful spectacle. The energy is infectious. The closer we got to the noise, the more the adrenaline raced through my veins.

The parade was already in progress by the time we found a spot on a crowded corner with a somewhat unobstructed view. I stood entranced by the sights and sounds surrounding me. As far as the eye could see, throngs of people were lined up on each side of the street. They were also above us on rooftops, hanging out of windows and crowding onto balconies.

The glittering floats each acted as its own huge boombox blasting the music of Madonna, Cher, Britney, and other gay icons while men, women, drag queens, leather daddies, and nearly naked boys gyrated while waving and tossing out candy, colorful beads, or bags of condoms and lube to anyone close enough to catch. I made it my mission to catch anything being tossed to the crowd that day. I learned the key was to try to catch the eye of someone on the float so they would throw the freebies directly to me. By the end of the day, I had more beads than I could wear and enough condoms and lube to last for months. I happily used them all!

One float after the other passed in front of us. They represented local bars, clubs, stores, and organizations. Between the floats were marching bands, line dancing cowboys, rifle brigades, politicians sitting in convertibles, drag queens dressed in balloons, men twirling batons in formation, and large groups of allies marching for organizations like PFLAG carrying signs reading things like "I love my trans son!" or "I love my lesbian daughter and her wife" or "My son is gay and so am I!" Large corporations were represented by employees marching in large groups carrying the banner of their company. I was impressed and encouraged that major corporations were comfortable showing their support.

If there wasn't already enough sensory overload, I heard a deafening roar of engines coming our direction. I could see a formation of motorcycles zig-zagging in formation with their powerful engines revving so loudly you could feel the vibrations. I've never been impressed by loud engines. As they drew closer I expected to see a bunch of tattooed leather daddies on these powerful machines. But to my surprise, as they circled in front of me I saw a flag which read dykes on bikes. These lesbians on their bikes were the fiercest women I had ever seen. Strong, fearless, women both black and white, butch and femme dressed in their finest leather, harnesses, and rainbow boas. Some smiled, some waved, some held up fingers and made a variety of gestures sure to elicit a crowd response. Many of them had their girlfriend riding on the seat behind them. I stood in amazement, certain that these were the most powerful, unapologetic women I had ever seen. I couldn't help but be impressed. Despite the noise, I heard myself hollering in approval along with the crowd.

I found myself in tears as open and affirming religious groups and churches marched proudly with signs declaring their support of their LGBTQ members and the community. Not just one church, but many passed by that day. Gay couples pushing children in strollers waving small rainbow flags marched passed. Smiling politicians with their supporters handed out buttons and magnets. Drag queens in competition sashes and sparking crowns sat on the back of convertibles waving gracefully. Police, firefighters, and members of the military passed us arm in arm with their partners. Trans elders led groups of younger trans people down the street waving their trans colors and carrying signs declaring their pronouns.

The parade lasted hours. The crowd never lost interest. We alternated between the parade route and an occasional visit back to the apartment for a snack and drink refill. Sometime in the late afternoon, the final parade entry passed followed by street cleaners who immediately began breaking down the barriers and cleaning up the colorful debris in the street. The streets and sidewalks emptied into the bars and restaurants where the party was just beginning and would last long into the wee hours of the morning.

Since that memorable day in Chicago I have attended Pride celebrations in Seattle, South Bend, Indianapolis, and Kansas City. Yes, as described by the preachers, there were plenty of gyrating, nearly naked men present. There was plenty of sex-positive imagery and activities. Gay pride is definitely a bawdy, colorful, gender-bending affair. I love it! It is a celebration of freedom, expression, and acceptance. At that first Pride I took plenty of pictures of the sexy men in their underwear dancing on the floats, but when all was said and done, it wasn't the skin that inspired me. It was the unabashed freedom to be who you are that brought tears to my eyes and fanned the flame of courage inside me.

I'm happy to now say I've walked the streets of gay neighborhoods in cities all over the USA. I've been in gay bars, nightclubs, bathhouses, and gay strip clubs. I've seen and done it all, so-to-speak. It has been a journey of permission, freedom, and expression. I love and embrace my community and our self-expression. I don't believe that gay men are more sexual than heterosexual people. I believe that gay men are simply happy to embrace and celebrate their sexuality instead of hide it and pretend it doesn't exist.

I was still young to the concept of freedom. It wasn't that many years earlier, while I was still going through what would be the final sessions of ex-gay therapy, that I found solace in a song by the Brooklyn Tabernacle Choir. The words to "This is How it Feels to be Free" stirred a longing in me.

> This is how it feels to be free
> This is what it means to know that
> I am forgiven
> This is how it feels to be free
> To see that life can be more than I imagined
> This is how it feels to be free

At the time I was imagining that life would begin when I was no longer gay if I could just stick with ex-gay therapy long enough. Instead of freedom, I only found discouragement and defeat.

After coming out to myself and God, there was no dramatic announcement to the world or anyone else. I simply began oozing out of the closet and timidly venturing into gay spaces. The only images of gay bars I had were from watching the TV series *Queer As Folk*. It gave me a window into the world I had only heard described to me by those who hated gays. The clubs in the TV series were sophisticated, glossy, and enormous. At the fictional club, the characters of the show were always surrounded by beautiful, extremely fit, young, gay men. Nearly naked go-go dancers gyrating on boxes scattered around the club. The dark hallways and bathrooms were lined with men making out and groping one another. I couldn't wait to experience this kind of gay utopia.

I quickly learned that South Bend was nothing at all like *Queer As Folk*. Truman's was far from glossy. It was an old brick warehouse with faded but gaudy rainbows and pink triangles painted on the outside. I wondered why it had to be so...gay. The first floor was the drag queen performance area. Drag queens both intrigued and terrified me. I didn't understand drag culture. *Why would men want to dress up like women? Were these glamorous and sexy women actually men? How could a man look that beautiful?* The drag show hostess was known simply as Bradley. She was crass with sharp wit. She didn't try to be believable as a woman. Her legs were hairy and her bulging crotch was always visible. No taping or tucking for Bradley. She was the "hostess with the mostess". She excelled at entertaining the crowd and making straight people uncomfortable. She could always spot the newbie who wanted to be incognito - something impossible while Bradley was in charge. She would tease and flirt endlessly once she found them.

I watched this happen and was terrified of being her next victim, so I spent most of my time upstairs near the dance floor that was in the middle of a large, high-ceiling room. While it was bathed in colorful lights and disco balls, the outside edges of the room were dark and easy to blend into. Sometimes I was recognized by a few men I had chatted with on Gay.com. They struck up conversations with me and we began to get acquainted. It felt very awkward because I was sort of in the closet and yet here I was sitting in a gay bar being flirted with. It wasn't Club Babylon from *Queer As Folk* but I was enjoying it. As I made friends, they would pull me onto the dance floor despite my objection because I was sure I must look like a fool. Truman's became a Saturday night ritual. I looked forward to it all week long.

One night early in my coming out journey I went to Truman's, ordered water from the bar and found a dark table where I could see but not be seen. I sipped my water (because I was still afraid to drink alcohol for fear I'd be instantly drunk) and people watched while nodding my head to the dance music. The songs were familiar to everyone else, but it was an entirely new-to-me songbook. I had been to Truman's enough to recognize a few favorite songs that while I didn't know the artist, title, or lyrics, I knew they made me want to dance. The liberation of being on the dance floor was euphoric. My parents didn't even allow us to clap to songs, let alone dance.

There I was, by myself, moving my body in complete abandon on the dance floor. I won't call it dancing because I'm sure it looked more like convulsing to a beat, but as I moved I felt a freedom unlike anything I had ever known. Due to my sheltered Baptist upbringing, I was only beginning to know some of the pop and dance music of over thirty years of life. Every song and artist was new to me. I knew the names Cher, Whitney, Madonna, and others, but I didn't recognize their voices or their songs. There was a complete disconnect between the celebrity names and their artistry.

Just as I went back to my seat, the DJ began a new track that I recognized from the handful of previous visits. I didn't know who the artist was but I recognized the infectious tune and knew I had to dance. I stepped into the light of the dance floor and thought, *Oh, I love this song! I wonder who it is?* As I let myself go, I listened more closely to the lyrics.

> *When you call my name it's like a little prayer*
> *I'm down on my knees, I wanna take you there*
> *In the midnight hour I can feel your power*

These lyrics seemed vaguely familiar to me. Perhaps it was the religious references and the choir in the background? It was a strange juxtaposition to hear sacred sounds on a strobe lit dance floor of a gay bar. I was drawn more deeply into the lyrics. I wanted to know them and the lyrical voice singing them. The song ebbed and flowed in an almost spiritual way. And then the instruments faded, the tempo slowed.

> *I hear your voice. It's like an angel sighing.*
> *I have no choice. I hear your voice.*

Feels like flying.

I bowed my head and swayed my body reverently, quietly singing along as best as I could recall these new-to-me lyrics.

> *Now I'm dancing*
> *It's like a dream*
> *No end and no beginning*
> *You're here with me it's like a dream*

In that moment, the crowded dance floor became an empty sanctuary that was all my own. I rocked my body to the music. I didn't care who might be watching me. I didn't care what I looked like. I was free. Free of fear, shame, and judgement. My dance was holy. It was like a prayer of gratitude and joy that here in *this* sanctuary I could be unashamedly me. I could dance and no one would stop me. I could dance with men and no one would condemn me. I could be whoever I wanted to be.

When the beat dropped and the music suddenly shifted from reverence to jubilation, I was awakened from my trance.

> *When you call my name it's like a little prayer*
> *I'm down on my knees, I wanna take you there*
> *In the midnight hour I can feel your power*
> *Just like a prayer you know I'll take you there*

I lifted my arms to the ceiling, but instead of the dark ceiling I saw a sunny, bright blue sky. With tears forming in my eyes, I danced as I had never danced before with complete, reckless abandon. It felt as if I were rising off the dance floor. I jumped. I gyrated. I clapped.

> *Just like a prayer, I'll take you there*
> *It's like a dream to me*
> *Just like a prayer*
> *Just like a prayer, your voice can take me there*

All my life I had examined music through a fundamentalist lens of judgement and fear. I was taught that the message of the song was the most important part of it. Music like this was blamed for the sinfulness of society. The lyrics of this song were religious, yet I knew they were sacrilegious too. I had become the controversy just by being me. I imagined how horrified the people who knew me as Pastor Barrett would be if they saw me dancing in a gay bar to this song obviously not about prayer.

Wait! This must be Madonna! I remember hearing about her and this song. It was very controversial!

I recalled religious people everywhere clutching their pearls when *Like A Prayer* was released. I remember hearing about her and her music from the pulpit. I didn't know what she sounded like, but I knew her music and videos were extremely controversial because of her unabashed sexual content and use of religious symbolism. I chuckled and blushed at my own ignorance. To everyone else there that night, it was just another night at Truman's. But to me it was church. I was godly and I was a sweaty, dancing, gay. And I was happier than I had ever been in my life.

As I drove home that night I realized, THIS is how it feels to be free!

I'm coming out
I want the world to know
Got to let it show
I'm coming out
I want the world to know
Got to let it show

–Diana Ross, "I'm Coming Out"

PRAYER

"No prayer, just real talk…"

CHAPTER 13
You Lied To Me

Dear Church,

 You gave me a place to belong. I gave you more than 30 years of my life. From the moment I was born, I was there for you. I eagerly participated in my Sunday School classes where we sang:

 Jesus loves the little children.
 All the children of the world.
 Red and yellow, black and white,
 They are precious in his sight.
 Jesus loves the little children of the world.

 You lied to me when you failed to mention that some were more precious in his sight than others. The black and brown children were only precious if they assimilated into our white culture. The LGBTQ children were only precious if they weren't LGBTQ. You lied to me.

 You told me that I was perfectly made in God's image, but when you found out I was gay, you told me I was broken and an abomination. You told me everyone was welcome at the church, but you didn't tell me they had to change to be like everyone else if they planned to stay there. You told me church was a safe, and loving place but you didn't tell me that love was conditional. You didn't tell me that it was only safe for those who complied.

You told me that church was our family. You celebrated that. My childhood photos are full of images of you and I spending time together with my entire family, smiling and dressed in the clothing you loved to see us in. "Only the best for the King of Kings" you told us. My mom and sister in pretty, modest dresses. My Dad, brothers and me in suits and ties. We marched down to the front of the church every Sunday and sat within the first three rows to receive what you had to give us.

You were my life. You were my friend. You were my teacher. You were my inspiration. You were my mentor. I trusted you. I listened to your every word. I respected you. I followed you.

You gave me a home, a church home as it was referred to. We spent Sunday morning, Sunday night, Wednesday night, and Thursday night with you each week. We came together for special week-long revival services and missionary conferences. We attended special services throughout the year like the New Year's Eve Watchnight Service and all night prayer meetings. Our time together was full of teaching, preaching, and singing praises to God. I loved singing your songs, directing the choir, teaching the classes, and ministering to the members.

I sometimes grew weary of the level of commitment expected by you, but you said it was little to ask in return for a God who had given his only son to die for our sins, so I complied. "God created you for His glory.

You were made to serve him. No sacrifice is too great for the one who gave His all for you." Well...when you put it like that, I guess I should have done more.

You told me that the community we built was the Family of God and what we had was exceptional. Those who weren't a part of this exclusive family of God longed for what we had. The euphoria we felt in a stirring praise and worship service was supernatural. "What you're feeling in here today" the preacher would say, "That's the Spirit of God. You won't find this anywhere else but in the House of God. This is what people out in the world are searching for." You lied to me.

I later learned that community can be built anywhere over common interests. It's not supernatural, it's actually quite natural and not difficult to attain when good people get together and intentionally share themselves. You lied to me. I've since felt that same feeling at a dinner party with friends, at a Janet Jackson concert, in a coffee shop having a conversation with a friend, at a Gay Pride parade, or on the crowded dance floor of a gay bar twirling to Whitney Houston's, "I Wanna Dance With Somebody".

You gave me a book called The Bible. You told me it was the inspired, inerrant, unchanging, living word of God and the final authority. You asked that I read, study, and memorize it daily. You promised rewards in the form of undefined "blessings" if I complied. You promised that it would make me feel really good and help me make better choices in life. If I had a problem, the Bible would show me how to fix it. With the Bible as your source, you taught me what to think, how to look, what to say and not say, who to be friends with, how to feel, how to behave, what music to listen to, how to dress, what to embrace and what to shun, who to ... it was almost like a magic eight ball. I learned from you that following the book's instructions would even give me life after death. All I had to do was pray a prayer and my eternal destiny was set. You promised that all of life's questions were answered in this holy book if I was willing to prayerfully read and search with an open heart to what God wanted to say to me. He would literally speak to me from this book if I was listening. It would guide my every step.

   You didn't tell me that everyone would interpret and apply it differently. You didn't tell me that when you said to believe the literal interpretation of the Bible that you don't actually take the entire Bible literally, but instead cherry picked what best suits the belief of the day. What fits is to be taken literally; what doesn't fit is to be taken figuratively. The things you don't understand, you mark up to cultural differences of the day when it was written or the mysterious ways of God that aren't meant to be known or understood. You didn't tell me that every major Christian denomination follows the same book and yet each believe and practice something quite different. Each thinks they are the most right too. You didn't tell me that the Bible was used to justify racism, sexism, slavery, killing people, homophobia, and a long list of other hateful practices. You used the book against me like a deadly weapon.

You gave me a messenger and you called him the Man of God. He was to be respected and listened to. He was our pastor and we looked up to him as an authority. He was God's anointed shepherd of the flock. He led, taught, and advised us. I drank up the preacher's words pouring from the pulpit because you said he was "God's man" and I should listen carefully to him. You told me to respect him. You didn't tell me he was just a man who claimed to speak for God. You didn't tell me he would say and do abusive and hateful things from the pulpit in order to manipulate people into doing what he wanted. He would mock and shame those like me. He would manipulate me into making life-changing decisions as a little boy who wasn't mentally mature enough to understand the weight of his decisions. You lied to me.

You asked a lot of me. Frankly, your requests felt more like rules and requirements, but you promised so many good things in return that I gladly submitted to you. You weren't hesitant to point out what was wrong in my life - in fact, that's pretty much all you did. It was all presented as the way to please God, be blessed, and earn rewards in heaven some day. You strongly exhorted me to make any sacrifice it took to experience a fulfilled Christian life and understand what true peace and joy were. You told me that only Christians could experience true peace and joy by surrendering to God. You told me that when I followed the rules - which were many and varied significantly from church to church - I would experience God's blessings in my life and He would use me for His glory. If I rejected these rules, I was rebellious and self-serving. My rebellion was blocking God's blessings in my life and could result in judgement and ultimately death. If God couldn't use me, then I was a hindrance to his work and might be eliminated from this Earth. You warned me of longing for worldly things like Lot's wife who, after turning back to take a final look at her burning home town was turned into a pillar of salt and left to crumble. You told me not to be distracted by the shiny trinkets Satan held up to lure me away from God because they were temporary and fleeting at best. Ultimately they will only bring you misery and harm, you told me. You lied to me.

"Sin will take you farther than you want to go, keep you longer than you want to stay, and cost you more than you want to pay!" the preacher would admonish.

The people out in the world were described as wandering through life aimlessly with no moral compass trying in vain to find ways to fill the "god-shaped void" inside them. This is why they turned to drugs, alcohol, sex, addictive behaviors, and other instant gratifications. "They might look happy, but don't be fooled; they are merely enjoying the pleasures of sin for a season" the preacher would say, "and when that seasons ends, they will find themselves standing before God empty handed with only wasted years and regrets to show for a life lived apart from God." You lied to me.

You gave me a direct line to God called prayer. You told me the more I prayed the closer I would get to God, and the closer I got to God the more clearly I would hear his voice. Volumes were written about how to pray, how long to pray, when to pray, and what to pray for. You encouraged me to spend hours on my knees in prayer. I was to pray about everything - literally everything. If I misplaced my keys, I would stop and pray and ask God to help me find my keys. When I found my keys, I would stop and thank God for answering my prayer and tell others "Praise the Lord! God answers prayer!" I would tell others, "God is good. I prayed and He helped me find my keys. God answers prayer!" You made it seem like God was some sort of magic genie in a bottle that when rubbed just right, he might grant me my wish. What you didn't tell me was that nearly every religion, belief system, and culture has something similar to prayer. Today when I misplace my keys, I stop and calmly center myself, retracing my steps in my mind and ... guess what? I always find my keys. My brain always knew where I left my keys, I just had to access that part of my brain to find them. Prayer isn't magical, it's simply centering yourself. It has been decades since I prayed to God. My life is rich and full and sometimes I misplace things and I find things. You lied to me.

You gave me a God. A God who was one yet three: God the Father, God the Son, and God the Holy Spirit. Each was separate yet one. You told me that God was all powerful and all knowing. He could do anything. He could even move mountains if I just believed. You told me all I had to do is have the faith of a mustard seed. If I wasn't receiving the answers I needed I just had to pray harder, surrender more, and love God more deeply. I could do all things! I could overcome anything and live victoriously. Yet you never told me what that actually looked like. How would I know? You told me I was to live in fear of God and his judgement if I didn't obey and please Him. He loved me, but would kill me if I didn't love Him back. You used Bible stories to remind me of the wrath of God unleashed on innocent people in order for him to get what he wanted. He created heaven for those who obeyed Him and hell for those who didn't. He allowed horrible things in order to test and strengthen me. He allowed evil in order to show his holiness. None of this made sense to me. It sounded like an abusive relationship, but I trusted it was best to follow this God of love who felt far from loving to me. You lied to me.

You told me he gave me his son Jesus who came and died for my sin. Yet the message of Jesus didn't match the message of the Church. Jesus hung out with people like me. He preached love and peace. We celebrated his death. We sang happy songs about his blood in church. We pretended to drink his blood and eat his flesh in communion. We asked "Are you washed in the blood of the lamb?" We glorified the bloody sacrifices of the Old Testament which were symbolic of Jesus' bloody demise while we feared and condemned the bloody rituals of other "false" religions and called them satanic and evil.

You told me the Trinity included the Holy Spirit who would mysteriously and vaguely speak to me via my heart and provide direction, affirmation, peace, and most importantly, convict me of my sin. You told me I could never trust myself because my heart was deceitfully wicked, so I needed to try to find my answers from God and his will which was very difficult to discern. The Holy Spirit would help me with this. I would know when I was following the Holy Spirit when I was filled with a peace that passed all understanding. That peace was ONLY given by God. No one else had that peace. That peace brought fulfillment and joy. You lied to me.

You warned me that if I ever strayed from what you taught me that I would be miserable. I would never know peace, joy, or fulfillment. I would make bad decisions. I would experience the judgement of God. I might lose my health, my children, my career and anything else meaningful to me. I spent years living in fear of this. You lied to me.

My mother told me when I was a little boy I would misquote, "The Lord is my shepherd, I shall not want."

Instead I quoted it as "The Lord is my shepherd and I don't want any." It wasn't a mistake, it was prophetic.

Church, you lied to me.

You LIED to me.

YOU LIED TO ME.

I don't want you anymore.

Finally Free from You,
Joel

PERMISSION

When you don't have a prayer.

CHAPTER 14
Godly AND Gay

This is the point in my story where people usually ask me questions like:

"So, are you still a Christian?"

"Do you still go to church?"

"Are you religious?"

I understand these inquiries and why people want to know. But when people ask me these types of questions, I always feel a sense of underlying anticipation that I'm going to say something like: "And then I made up with God, found the magic Bible verses to assure me God loves gays, and now my husband and I are active members of an open, affirming, and welcoming church where we sing in the choir and hang out with our church family praising God together." This is the happy ending that many well-meaning Christians want to hear. I believe it's because it wraps everything up nicely with a pretty bow that feels like, "See? All things *do* work together for good!" in the way that makes people feel secure in their own faith.

My faith has both devolved and evolved since I came out. After decades of being taught the unquestionable absolutes of the Bible, Christianity, and God I found the courage to question it all. I put it all to the test. I no longer find security in the black and white but embrace the beautiful gray of uncertainty. People are often uncomfortable with me being comfortable *not* knowing. The truth is, faith isn't faith if it can all be explained. If it all fits neatly into a pretty, little "God box" then does it really require any faith at all? If God can neatly fit into my theological box, is God really big enough to be my God?

"But how do you justify your life without the Bible?" is the typical next question. There are entire theological libraries written about the subject of homosexuality from all points of view and what the Bible does or doesn't say about it. I have good friends who are scholars and activists who have devoted their life's work to challenging the church's theology in regards to this. I love that they do this important and restorative work but I leave that work to them. When I meet people who want to have theological discussions or have serious questions about what the Bible really says, I refer them to those resources like *Walking the Bridgeless Canyon* by Kathy Baldock and Matthew Vines' important work *God and the Gay Christian*. I know my Bible very well, especially all the passages related to homosexuality. I could argue and debate with the best of them, but I don't. I have no need to point to Bible passages to justify or defend who I am.

I assure you, I am not a bitter gay. I'm not anti-God, anti-faith, or anti-religion. If you are a part of a faith community that is feeding your spirit and helping you become a better person, by all means - please continue participating in that. I would never discourage you from feeding your spiritual self. However, if you are a part of something that tears you down and tells you that who you are is broken, sinful, and destined for God's wrath, then please love yourself enough to leave that toxic environment.

I wasted decades of my life trying to please "God", praying fervently and desperately seeking his will to avoid making a wrong move. It never occurred to me how insulting that was to the creator who had given me all I needed to be all that I could be. Looking back I realize how absurd and limiting this mindset was. If I am God's prize creation, made in His image, the Bride of Christ, then surely I've been given what I need to be all that He created me to be. A tree doesn't have to beg God to show it how to be a tree. It doesn't have to seek God's will about how tall, wide, or deep it should grow. It doesn't ask permission to bloom in the spring or shed its leaves in the fall. By its very existence it has been given all that it needs to be the tree it is supposed to be. It's all right here inside the tree. Why would I be any different? I am a part of this same universe of life. I have all I need to be me. I am not insufficient or broken. This comforting knowledge empowers me and gives me the confidence to be who I am.

Today I don't pray in the way that I used to. In fact, the word "prayer" is uncomfortable for me. Instead, I have conversations with myself. Now, that might sound funny to you, but it's all part of the faith that I identify with today. I now identify as a faitheist. Yes, you read that right, a **Faitheist**. A coaching client of mine introduced me to this name she coined for herself. (Thank you Ann!) I knew instantly that it described me more perfectly than any descriptor I had ever tried on. I am not atheist. I am not agnostic, I'm not deist. I'm a faitheist.

What does this mean to me? It means I believe. I believe there is more to this universe than meets the eye. I believe we are all a part of and interconnected to something bigger than this physical world. I believe that what we know sheds very little light on what we do not know because it is beyond our comprehension. I don't try to define or explain what we do not know. I choose not to name or worship any of this. I don't need a human prescribed theology to guide me. I believe I've been given all that I need to be the best possible me. I am not lacking. I believe It is my responsibility to live my life in respect of all of this. I don't live for an afterlife, I live for the only reality any of us know for sure: this moment. I don't seek a house of worship. Instead, I find "church" in unexpected places with unsuspecting people. When my spirit has been fed, I know I've been to church.

Do I live in fear that I might be wrong? No. Not one bit. All those years I believed by faith everything that was taught. I saw the inconsistencies. I had questions, but I feared to ask them. Instead, I accepted my reality as the safest and best option despite my questions.

The 2004 movie *The Village* by M. Night Shyamalan still resonates with me today as the best allegorical portrayal of how I once lived. Spoiler Alert: In the movie, which appears to be set in the 1700s, the characters live in a small, rectangular village in a clearing surrounded by a dense, dark forest on all four sides. The residents have been told that they are only safe inside the compound. They must never wander beyond the well-defined perimeter where "those we do not speak of" dwell. The respected leaders explain that the village has an ancient, unspoken agreement with the unseen creatures in the dark woods. The creatures will protect the village from harm as long as the villagers do not venture into their territory. The village lives in fear of the creatures they have never seen. On occasion, eerie sounds come from the forest to remind the village of the doom that waits them should they stray from the safe place. A series of events leads a young woman named Ivy to venture out far beyond the compound where she encounters great risk and danger as she travels through the woods. Eventually she discovers a wall, climbs over it and finds herself standing next to a modern paved road in the present day. The viewer and Ivy slowly realize that everything they had been led to believe was not reality. The village wasn't ancient. There were no monsters in the woods. The compound wasn't the safe place they believed it to be. It didn't protect them, it controlled and confined them. But it was only when Ivy had the courage to put it all to the test, ask the hard questions, face her fears, and challenge herself that she discovered true freedom.

The first time I watched The Village it felt autobiographical. I remembered how trustingly I accepted what was presented to me as the only truth. I also remember feeling frustrated with the pat answers I was given to honest questions about things that didn't seem to add up for me. I always had a healthy skepticism, but I was afraid to venture outside the compound. It seemed safer to simply "have faith" as they would say. "We'll understand it better by and by" and "farther along, we'll know all about it." the old gospel songs promised. It always bothered me that questioning God or testing one's faith was discouraged. If I don't put what I believe to the test, how do I know it holds up? When it comes to my faith, I put it all to the test. I questioned it all. I faced my fears. I did the unthinkable. I took a fresh look at everything. I embraced the unknown.

Over the years I've watched many documentaries about cults and other abusive religious environments. I have been repeatedly struck by how familiar they always feel to me. I'm shaken by how easily humans can accept what is presented as truth without question. One of the hallmarks of a cult is skillfully weaving truth into a false reality so that it ALL seems like truth. Ex-gay therapy did this masterfully.

Today I don't live as a captive of fear. Thank God I have that peace that passes all understanding and distresses those who believe I couldn't possibly have peace. Perhaps you're surprised I credited God. I never said I don't believe in God. But I don't believe in the God I was taught because that one is too small, insufficient, and man-made. I've discovered something much bigger than the God we kept in our little clearly-defined, Baptist box.

Faith-e-ist

noun

One who has faith in something greater than the human existence and believes there is more than meets the eye and the interconnectivity of the universe but does not choose to identify, name, or worship that belief but rather live life in respect of that.

I am a faitheist and I've never been more at peace.

It's okay not to know all the answers. It's better to admit our ignorance than to believe answers that might be wrong. Pretending to know everything, closes the door to finding out what's really there.

— Neil deGrasse Tyson

PRAYER

"All the world's a stage, and all the men and women merely players; they have their exits and their entrances…"

CHAPTER 15
All the World's a Stage

You are a player in this stage production we call life. Never underestimate the power of your role in the lives of others. Sometimes that is an active, speaking role, sometimes you're a walk-on and sometimes a co-star. I wouldn't be where I am today if it weren't for the many people who played a role in my story. Many of them are unaware of the impact they had. Some were allies. Some were LGBTQ family. Some were strangers whose names are unknown to me. Some were friends and family. Some became chosen family. Many came from unexpected places.

I will introduce you to some of these very impactful people. Why? Because I want to inspire you to consider what role you play in the lives of those around you. What do you do or say when you meet someone like me on the early part of their journey? How can you make a difference in their life? This is not an acknowledgements list, but rather an inspiration list.

"One of the most powerful forms of activism is simply being who you are, wherever you are."

--David Seymour (my husband)

The Couple

When I was a young teenager, the church we attended would go to a nursing home once a month on a Sunday afternoon to hold services for the residents. The service included a favorite old hymn sing-along followed by special music - usually my mother and I singing a duet. The pastor would preach a sermon and then we would socialize with the "old folks" as we referred to them. During that socializing time I would often wander around the sunny, high ceilinged common space filled with plants and a fish tank near the entrance to watch the fish. More than once I observed an older lesbian couple come in to visit some friend or relative. To me, they seemed to be the same age as the residents of the home. I was fascinated by them and studied them closely. I had never seen anyone like them before. They were both impeccably dressed every time I saw them. One was always wearing a fitted, colorful, Sunday dress complete with coordinating jewelry, shoes, and sometimes a hat with her silver curls falling beneath it. Her bright smile was always framed by freshly painted, ruby red lips. She was the very picture of the quintessential woman of her generation. Today she might be referred to as a lipstick lesbian. The other half of the couple always wore a tailored suit and tie. She sported a short cropped hairstyle and walked with a casual jaunt that reminded me of Fred Astaire. At a glance one would assume she was he - and perhaps today she might use he/him pronouns, or perhaps she was what some would refer to as a butch lesbian.

But it wasn't just their snappy attire that caught my attention, it was the way they carried themselves so unashamedly and confidently. They always entered arm in arm with smiles on their faces calling out friendly greetings to familiar faces as they walked down the hall to visit whoever they came to see. They were completely comfortable in their own skin. They seemed to be well-known and well-liked. Their joyful energy was undeniable. I could feel it from a distance. I knew there was something special about them, but it confused me because I was told it was not possible to have what they had and be "living in sin". I saw them numerous times. I have no idea who they were nor is it likely they ever noticed the awkward young teenager studying them. My mother mentioned them once in disgust and pity as we drove away. I filed them away in my brain as just one example of someone boldly and happily living their truth. It didn't add up to what my parents and the church taught me and I liked that. Deep inside, I too, was a questioning rebel.

The Shirtless Runner

When I turned sixteen I got my first job at McDonald's. Effingham was a small enough town that you felt you sort of knew, or at least recognized everyone who lived there. If someone new came to town, they stood out. I was working the front register one day when the most beautiful, striking man I had ever seen got in my line. He was tall, very fit, bronze-skinned and probably in his late twenties. His perfect hair was cut and styled like George Michael's and included blonde highlights. In his right ear he had small earring which was scandalous in small town America. All the employees were a-buzz. "Who is this beautiful man? He has an earring! Is he gay?" I was so naive that until this was mentioned, it hadn't occurred to me that he was probably gay.

My heart leapt at the possibility. "Which ear is it in?" someone asked. "Because you know what they say, 'Left is right and right is wrong!'" someone chimed in. That meant if a man wore an earring in his left ear it was a fashion statement but if it was in his right ear it meant he was gay. While there was no truth to this urban myth, at the time it was a common belief. He stuck out like a sore thumb in conservative Effingham. No one looked like this. After his first visit to McDonald's I started spotting other places. Often I'd see him jogging shirtless wearing nothing but tiny jogging shorts and a gold chain. I drank in every inch of his muscular body and filed it away for use later. I also noted the courage he had to be authentically himself in a community that undoubtedly judged, mocked, and harassed him. He must have been in Effingham on a short term job detail of some sort because he was only there for a few months and then he was gone. I never knew his name or anything else about him. He has no idea the impact he had on this young, closeted, gay teen who was afraid to admit how attracted he was to that handsome stranger.

The Co-worker

Not all the influencers in my life were nameless. I could never forget the name Rollin A. Duckwitz, III. He was an eye-catching young man my age and height who walked into McDonald's one day and with a noticeable, dramatic flair handed me his completed application for employment. His spiked, bleached blonde hair, stereotypical way of speaking, and flamboyant style immediately set him apart from the usual teenage boys in our small town. He gave me a broad smile and exited the restaurant. My curious eyes followed his swish until he was out of sight. *I like that guy.* I passed his application on to the hiring manager with a recommendation that they call him for an interview. A week later, I walked into work and there stood Rollin wearing the ugly, polyester uniform in a hideous color that could only be described as very, very burnt orange. No one looked good in that uniform, but he came closest.

Rollin was the first gay person I knowingly met. He never announced he was gay, but everyone just knew he was. He made no effort to suppress himself or hide who he was. He was outgoing and funny with a larger than life drag-queen personality. In 1983 this was very unusual for a teenage boy, especially in rural Illinois. I secretly admired his confidence and fearlessness. After the initial whispers and gossip Rollin quickly endeared himself to everyone he worked with. I longed to know more about him. *What was his life really like? Do his parents know? Why does everyone seem to like him despite him being gay?*

I was afraid to get too close to Rollin for fear he would pick up on the secret that I was just like him. I'm sure he didn't need to get close to me to figure that out, but I didn't understand "gaydar" at that time in my life. I didn't have a crush on him, but I did have a deep interest in knowing more about the only gay person I knew in my small, sheltered, world.

High school graduation came and off to college I went. We never spoke again outside of one random encounter with him at a store while I was back home visiting my parents. That was the last time I ever saw Rollin. Since then I have often thought about him and wondered what became of him. He left an indelible mark on my life by boldly being himself, long before it was acceptable or even safe to do so. He has remained a source of inspiration to me all my life.

A few years ago an internet search revealed that Rollin passed away in January of 2015. The cause of death was not listed. The simple obituary listed his survivors and the many places he had worked over the years. It also stated that he would be cremated and there would be no services per his request.

This news deeply saddened me. I revisited his obituary several times hoping to see something I didn't notice the last time I read it. I found his profile on Facebook and skimmed through the few public posts hoping to learn more about his life. I learned he liked cats, but nothing more. With regret I wondered why I hadn't searched for him on Facebook earlier.

I don't know what I was looking for. I guess I wanted to catch up on the last thirty years of silence. I think I wanted validation for the happy, fulfilled life I had created in my mind for Rollin. I imagined him moving to a progressive city out west somewhere. I imagined the wonderful man who he shared his life with in a community where he was loved and appreciated for the vivacious person he was. I imagined that one day we would unexpectedly connect again and I could share with him the influence that he was in my life and thank him for the empowerment he unknowingly gave to me. I imagined we would laugh about my closeted youth and fascination for him. I imagined he would smile and say "I always knew you were gay, Joel." We would laugh at my naivety. I Imagined I would introduce him to my husband and it would be the start of long distance friendship for years to come.

None of this can happen now. Rollin will never know the influence he has had in my life all these years. I don't know why he left his world at the young age of 48, but I regret not being able to share with him my gratitude for the gift he gave me. God only knows how many, like myself, were silently watching from behind the closet door and finding hope and inspiration from him.

The College Friend

While attending the tiny, conservative, fundamentalist Trinity Baptist College in Jacksonville, Florida I met Gloria Swardenski, now Gloria Kane. Even though the school was small, our paths rarely crossed. I was a dorm student and she was a married student who lived with her husband off campus. She and I knew each other, but not well. It was the beginning of what we have often called our parallel lives. After college, we both ended up living in Peoria, Illinois. She and her husband attended the church where I was associate pastor. Our children were born around the same time. Our kids played together. Our families became close. When I moved to Indiana to start the North Pointe Baptist Church, Gloria and her husband also moved to Indiana. As I was starting the church, Gloria was starting her coaching business. Life coaching was a new concept to me at that time. She asked if I would be willing to be her first client so she could get her coaching hours in and become better at her craft. Little did either of us know what that was going to mean for both of us. With each phone call our friendship deepened. We were both questioning the value of so much of what we were taught in our upbringing. In keeping with our parallel lives, both our marriages ended about the same time. Gloria played such a pivotal role in my story. I was distrustful of church people because church had proven to be the least safe place to be real. When I finally summoned the courage to tell her who I really was she simply listened, accepted me, and loved me even more deeply. As time went on, I shared every secret with her and she with me. Today we remain kindred spirits.

There are two powerful questions Gloria asked me during those pivotal moments of my life. I revisit these questions often and now use them in my own coaching practice. When I expressed my concern of family and friends finding out I was gay she asked in her simple, straightforward manner:

"What are you afraid of?"
I had to think through that for a moment. I had never really put words to this particular fear.

"I'm afraid of everyone rejecting me and losing all my friends and family."

"Okay." she replied. "So what's the worst that could happen?"

"Well, I'd lose everyone and have no one."

"So, then what would you do?" She asked.

"I guess I'd have to build new relationships."

"Could you do that?"

I thought about this for a moment."Yes, I think I could."

That simple series of questions helped me realize that despite all I feared, I still had options. I could do this. I was also encouraged at the prospect of not trying to please those people who I doubted loved me for who I was anyway. I could let go of them and find people who would accept me as I am.

The truth is, I did lose just about everyone from my past life. Some, like my sister, dropped me as soon as I admitted I had homosexual desires. Others stayed around because I was in conversion therapy and they were willing to support me while getting help as long as I ultimately quit being gay. Once they realized I wasn't going to ever be straight, they cut me out of their lives too. While it bothered me that people who I thought loved me could so easily erase me from their lives with little to no conversation or attempt to understand me, I also found it very liberating. It didn't cause me the pain I expected. It was like the greatest clarity ever began settling in. *I don't want or need these people in my life because they don't actually love me.* It wasn't all that difficult for me to build new friendships and choose my family, because I discovered that authentic people are attracted to authenticity. The more comfortable I became being Joel - just as I am, with no apology or hiding - people liked me better. My relationships got stronger, deeper, and more meaningful. Judgmental people don't know how to handle someone confidently living their life so they tend to retreat. I learned that I didn't care what those people from my past thought or said about me. Some tried to "love me back to Christ" with syrupy words, tears, and deep concern. I often refer to it as hating me with the love of Christ. I think it It bothers them deeply that my life doesn't bother me.

Gloria helped me dismantle my fear of what others might think and the fear of losing those people. I quit giving them my power. Gloria and I talk regularly. We have been there for each other through all the ups and downs of our lives. She is one of the unexpected gifts of my past who continues to play a major role in my life. All I can say is, "I love you, my sister!"

The Pastor

I was done with church after so many damaging experiences and living with the constant judgement of being me. Someone told me there was a church in downtown Elkhart, Indiana that was LGBT welcoming and affirming. I couldn't imagine what that must be like but I decided to try it out. I sat in the pew listening to Pastor Anne deliver the morning sermon. It was the first time I had ever heard a woman preach. That was certainly not allowed in the churches I grew up in. I was intrigued by how foreign this United Church of Christ felt to me. It was nothing like the casual, evangelistic churches I knew. The liturgy, unfamiliar hymns, and broad theology were hard for me to follow, but I did my best. What made the greatest impact on me was looking around the sanctuary on a Sunday morning and seeing LGBTQ couples sitting arm in arm, singing in the choir, and serving in various capacities. I was amazed that not a single straight person in the room was blinking an eye. This was a reality beyond my imagination. Later that week I sat in Pastor Anne's office pouring my heart out to her. She listened with compassion and love. I don't remember our conversation but I remember that spending time with Anne made me feel that everything was somehow going to be okay. We met at a time when I was a struggling single dad trying to make ends meet. I felt like my world was nothing but chaos. Everything about Anne felt calm and ordinary, and I mean that as a compliment. I needed to see normalcy. She and her wife Tammie showed me that being gay can be as ordinary and comfortable as any other relationship. Anne was right. Everything is okay.

The Best Friend

It started in the chat room of Gay.com. I met a handsome stranger named Chris Hooper who became my best friend and gay mentor. Chris had been out pretty much all of his life. He fully embraced his gayness. He had seen and done it all and loved everything about gay culture. Chris was the best friend and brother I didn't know I was missing from my life. He and I couldn't have lived more polar opposite lives. We had little in common. He had lived life BIG and open and I had lived life small and sheltered. He listened to me. He cared about me. He loved me. He wanted the best for me. So Chris made it his mission to help me get integrated into this strange, new world, of gay culture. Like a *Gay for Dummies* book only in real time, he taught gay history to me including the importance of drag, iconic figures, events, the underground ballroom scene, and groundbreaking gay movies. He made a list of must-see movies for me that included: *Paris Is Burning, Priscilla, Queen of the Desert, Angels in America, Jeffrey* (which I still haven't watched) and many others. Chris always made it okay for me to be ignorant, but not to stay ignorant. He never made me feel silly for my ignorance or naïveté.

Chris and I are brothers from another mother. He loved me and mentored me. He and I are still best friends and brothers to this day.

The Coffee Shop Crew

One of the many jobs I had while struggling to get my footing after coming out was managing the Daily Grind in downtown Elkhart, Indiana. The owner Tanya Fox Bleiler created an atmosphere of community and acceptance amongst the employees as well as the customers. It was the first place of employment that felt safe enough for me to be out. I was able to explore what it meant and looked like for me to be gay in public in an environment that I knew would have my back if anything went wrong. As a newly-out gay man in his late 30s it was challenging for me to know what that meant for Joel. I was going through what many men who come out later in life describe as a second puberty. The freedom to dress how I wanted, listen to the music I wanted, watch what I wanted, and flirt with whoever I wanted was exhilarating to me. Thanks to Tanya I was able to explore who I was without fear of judgement. She and the entire team loved and supported me. She gave me the permission to express myself. Thanks to *The Daily Grind*, I met my husband, David.

The Walk-Ons

I'm hesitant to use the term walk-on because it feels demeaning, but that is not my intention. There have been so many people who have had a moment or two in my life where they will never know the impact of their presence in that moment.

I think of the assistant pastor Tom Hilliker who played the role of intently listening to me during my many times of chaos and crisis. He was there to look into my eyes and give me his undivided attention with love. He didn't offer answers or try to fix anything. He didn't judge me. He simply listened with compassion and would put a hand on my shoulder or a hug.

There were many walk-ons like Tom who offered a kind, well-placed word of encouragement, a hug, or a listening ear.

The Parents

My parents and I did not have a strong relationship. They were among the most harsh and judgmental people I have known in life. Even when I was the godly man in ministry, they had problems with my church not being conservative enough, the way I dressed, or the life choices I made for me and my family. There was always something they were concerned about. Trying to please them was a moving target. I eventually gave up.

They had an opinion about everything that included a scripture, sermon, and literature to back it up. After every visit with them, I would receive a letter that expressed their concern for what they observed while in my presence. This was BEFORE I resigned from my church, divorced my wife, and came out as gay. So you can imagine how well they handled that series of events.

My mother never came to terms with me being gay. Not many months after I came out to her she was diagnosed with early dementia/Alzheimer's. As the disease took more of her, any hope of a relationship was diminished until it eventually claimed her life.

I was an enigma to my father. He didn't know what to do with me nor how to relate to me. I was my mother's child. Unlike my much older brothers, I had no interest in sports, rough play, fixing things, building things or any of the other stereotypical "masculine" things he knew. The only thing we did together was work. He insisted that I know how to work, so through various projects around the house and yard he taught me to work. He was a man of few words. He rarely laughed. He rarely praised me unless it was about using my talents for God. He never said he was proud of me for anything. Probably because pride was a sin in his book.

My father was an extremely critical man who loved a good debate. As a first pressman in a printing company he had years of experience in looking for flaws in every piece of printed material that came off the press. He was no different about everyone and everything around him. He was quick to point out the faults, sins, and shortcomings of others—including me. I was always aware of my wrongs, but rarely aware of anything I was doing right. This taught me from a young age that Dad was not a safe space for me. I learned to share less and less with him so he would not have the opportunity to correct, criticize, admonish, and judge me. I kept a safe distance from him. I disliked him. He was prone to angry outbursts. He was stern. He was intimidating.

After coming out to him and Mom, it dissolved any remaining glue of our relationships and cut off all but a few casual conversations about the weather for the remainder of his life until the very end.

As my mother succumbed to Alzheimer's, it became evident that her time was rapidly approaching. I made the phone call to Dad.

"Dad, I know Mom isn't doing well and I'd like to see her before she passes. My partner David and I are driving down to see her and you tomorrow. We've booked a hotel and will be there tomorrow evening."

I slipped in the reference to David quite casually, hoping he wouldn't pounce on it and begin preaching at me. He didn't acknowledge it. I wondered if he had even heard what I said. *Did he understand what I meant when I referred to my partner David?*

This was the first time David's name had ever been mentioned in a conversation with Dad. I knew that he most likely had heard through my siblings or the grapevine that I was with a man but Dad and I didn't really talk unless absolutely necessary.

On the way to Effingham from South Bend, David and I wondered what our experience with Dad would be like. I was sure Dad - who was not shy of confrontation - would be very quick to share how disappointed he is in me, quote scripture and warn us of God's judgment for our horrible sinful life.

A few minutes before we arrived in my hometown, he called to ask if we could stop by the house before we went to our hotel. I agreed, but my heart began beating in a panic because I was certain this was his way of setting up a confrontation with us. I sat in fear and dread for the final leg of our trip.

When we arrived at the front door of his home, he opened the door with a big smile, embraced me warmly, and respectfully shook hands with David after I introduced him. We sat down in the large living room of my childhood home. Little about the house had changed over the years. He brought us a glass of water and sat down to talk. He asked about the grandchildren, my job, where I lived, and other mundane matters. He then turned to David and began asking him questions about his life, job, and upbringing. I barely heard the conversation. I sat in dreaded anticipation of the inevitable. I trembled inside as I turned my attention back to the subsiding conversation.

To my surprise, Dad seemed genuinely happy to have company in his home. The more he chatted with us, the more I let my guard down and began seeing something in him I had never seen before. He was lonely. He was isolated. He and Mom had spent their lives alienating most people from them because of their judgement and condemnation.

I saw my Dad through new eyes that night. I felt a sense of regret in him that I'd never seen before. He truly wanted to know me and the man I love. It wasn't simply a cordial meeting. It was as if he was saying, "I'm all alone in the world now and I realize I sacrificed my relationships for the sake of my principles and now I don't even know my own son."

For the first time in my life I felt empathy for my father. I saw his humanity. We talked for an hour or more and never once did he quote any scripture to us, express judgement for our "lifestyle", or say anything confrontational to us. I sat in shock. Who was this man? This is not the father I knew.

The hour was getting late and I could see he was getting tired. He was always an early to bed, early to rise person.

"Dad, thank you for having us over tonight. We're going to head to the hotel now. Why don't we meet for breakfast somewhere in the morning before heading over to mom's nursing home?"

What happened next was the most beautiful gift my father ever gave me. He motioned toward the ugly floral print sofa from my childhood and said, "You know, that sofa pulls out into a daybed. You're welcome to stay here tonight."

Time stopped. *Did my Dad just invite us to spend the night and share a bed in his home?! Did he really just say that?* Trying to hide our shock, David and I thanked him for his kind offer, but politely declined. As we said good night, Dad hugged us both and with tears in his eyes and a crack in his voice he said, "You're welcome in my home anytime."

That was the moment Dad accepted me. For the first time in my life, I was able to envision a relationship with him that was no longer built on what was wrong with me. *I love you Dad. I wish we had gotten to know one another before it was too late.*

A few short months after my Mom's funeral, I stood at my Dad's funeral service. There, in the church I grew up in, I stood in front of my siblings, family friends, and church members and shared this beautiful story of the most precious gift my Dad ever gave me.

All the world's a stage. We each have a role. Surrounding us are a cast of characters who need us more than even they realize. Before you make your moves and speak your lines, remember they may not remember what you said or did but they will remember how you made them feel.

There are places I'll remember
All my life though some have changed
Some forever, not for better
Some have gone and some remain

All these places have their moments
With lovers and friends, I still can recall
Some are dead and some are living
In my life I've loved them all

> —*John Winston Lennon / Paul James McCartney,*
> *"In My Life"*

PRAYER

"I don't want to do this for the rest of my life."

CHAPTER 16
I'm Out! Now What?

As I prepared to write this book, I had to carefully choose which parts of my life to include. I decided to focus on the portion of my life from childhood to coming out because it best represented my conflicted journey of living in fear and shame before coming out and living authentically. This is the story of godly ... but gay.

Limiting the book to this timeline means that there is little to no mention of events that occurred after my marriage ended, coming out to my children, and meeting my husband and other significant moments. I have worked hard in these pages to not tell anyone's story but my own. However, my story wouldn't be complete without filling in some of these details.

It is important to note that life got very foggy from the moment I reached out to Exodus International and the following years. The fog began slowly lifting around the time I met my husband. When I look back now, it can be difficult for me to piece together the precise timeline. It often feels as if everything that happened during that time was happening simultaneously, but in reality it was not. What I do remember very clearly is *what* happened and *how* I felt. I was in a long, dark, oppressive tunnel with no light at the end of it. I often wished for death and would have welcomed a swift end to my misery. I found myself fantasizing about ways I could die that wouldn't be suicide. I didn't exactly want to kill myself, but I wanted to be dead. *Maybe that car will hit me head on and I'd die instantly!* It seemed like the perfect answer for relieving all the weight I was carrying. *I feel bad that my children will grow up without a Dad but their Mom should find and marry someone better than me anyway. They'd all be better off without me.*

My life felt like a weight heavier than any human being should be required to bear. I was processing past, present, and future all at once. No stone was unturned. I was challenging every norm in my life which was throwing a huge wrench into the gears of the well-oiled machine of my existence. Everything I was accustomed to was jerking chaotically out of control and coming to a halting stop. I was out of control and terrified.

When I entered ex-gay therapy, I thought I had this one thing that I needed fixed and then I could move on. When I speak to audiences I point to a sunspot on my face that I wish wasn't there. I compare the beginning of my journey to this imaginary scenario. "Doctor, I feel really good about myself and my body. I think I've pretty much got my act together, but there's this one sunspot on my face that I'd like to have removed because it shouldn't be there." What I learn from the doctor as he goes to remove it is that it isn't just a freckle; it's a visible manifestation of a cancer that has spread throughout my entire body.

While this story is made up, it is how I felt when I took the first step to get honest with myself. I naively thought I was fixing this one troublesome thing about myself. I quickly discovered it wasn't one thing - it was all things. Like an onion, under every layer was another layer. I couldn't address part of me without addressing all of me. These are some of the layers of the onion that weren't addressed in other chapters in this book.

People often ask, "How did your wife react when you told her?" My response? "How do you think she reacted?!" No wife deserves to hear the news that her husband is gay. Is there really a right or wrong way to react to such news? It was one of the most difficult and shame-filled days of my life. Despite all of the challenges of our dysfunctional relationship, I didn't want to hurt her, but I knew I had to live in my truth which would definitely hurt her.

I remember one of her first questions was, "You never touched our children, did you?" This may sound extreme today, but it is still common for religious groups to equate homosexuality with pedophilia. I was disappointed that this even entered her mind, but I understood where it came from. She grew up in the same religious mess I did. It was what we had all been taught. When you believe that homosexuality is the sin of all sins then all evil is attached to it. Since I was still in the beginning stages of getting myself "fixed", we decided to stick it out and try to keep things together while I got help.

We spent the next 18 months attempting to salvage our marriage, but a new challenge emerged. As I made changes in my own life to try to become a healthier individual, it further exposed the codependent and dysfunctional nature of our relationship. It also revealed how badly I had neglected Joel for all of my life. I had never given myself permission to be me. I knew how to be a godly husband, father, and pastor, but I had no idea how to be the man named Joel. I spent my life denying myself the right to be acknowledged and punishing myself for being me. For the first time I was facing my fear and shame. While this empowered me, it only added stress and confusion to our marriage.

In our religious world, divorce was not just a disgrace, it was a sin. Marriage is a sacred commitment for life. *People look up to us. What will they think? What will they say? What about our children?* I didn't want to be a failure but it felt inevitable.

Ex-gay therapy required all of my mental and emotional strength. All my energy had to be devoted to me. There was very little leftover for anyone or anything else. Peeling back the layers of my dysfunctional life only exposed more pungent and painful layers that brought foreign emotions to me. I cried all the time, about everything. I felt everything. I had thrown open the doors to the locked closets of my heart and was shining light on the most painful parts of me. The pain was intense. More than once, I found myself on the floor writhing in a fetal position sobbing, unable to even put words to my pain.

Trying to pastor my church became an annoying distraction. The work that needed to be done on myself left no energy to give to the small congregation I pastored. I knew it would destroy the church if they found out what was really going on with me. I began contemplating resigning my church.

I came to a crossroads in life. I remember very clearly the day I stood looking out my bedroom window to the North Pointe Baptist Church across the street. I was proud of my work, but I was too distracted and exhausted to feel it on that rainy, fall day. As I reflected on my twelve years in ministry, I had a life-changing revelation.

I don't think I want to do this for the rest of my life. I thought this was going to be my life's work, but the thought of doing this for the rest of my life does not excite me. This has required so much from me. I've spent all these years investing in the lives of others and receiving little in return. My life is spent helping others live their best life, but in the process I'm missing out on my best life. There is so much that I would like to do and experience, but if I keep doing this, I'm going to wake up when I'm seventy and be filled with regrets. I don't want to just be starting at seventy. I want to live life, now.

As the rain dripped down the glass in front of me, I felt a surge of courage and resolve as I repeated the sentiment emphatically without the doubt.

I don't want to do this for the rest of my life.

Shortly thereafter I announced my resignation to my church. It was an emotional goodbye on the last Sunday I stood in that pulpit. I knew I wasn't just saying goodbye to this church, but I was saying goodbye to my career. I had no clue what was next. I couldn't imagine a life outside of ministry. It was all I had ever known and all I had ever studied and prepared for since that fateful day in church when I was eleven. I was finally going to be free from "full-time Christian service". I was not oblivious to the magnitude of this decision, but deep inside I was at peace. This was best for me. I was doing something for me. This was a new feeling. I liked it.

Had I known how incredibly difficult the next few years would be, I might have lost my courage to leave ministry. I ignorantly thought that all of the impressive things I had accomplished in my ministry career would impress any hiring manager reviewing my resume. I couldn't have been more naively wrong. No one knew what to do with a former pastor. My education and experience had no more value than the paper my resume was printed on. I spent the next several years working two, three, sometimes four jobs at once to piece together an income. At one point I was delivering pizza, working the front desk at a gym so I could have a gym membership, substitute teaching, and giving estimates for foundation and waterproofing repairs for a company owned by some friends of mine.

My ex-wife and I moved to a small, nearby town and enrolled our previously homeschooled kids in the public school. I continued to work numerous jobs and attend ex-gay therapy sessions, but something was changing inside me. I was getting acquainted with me and I liked who I saw. I also learned that the more authentically I lived the more fulfilling life became. Freedom felt so much better than fear. I started catching a vision for a reality that never seemed possible before. Maybe I could live happily as a gay man. Around the time I quit ex-gay therapy, my wife and I split up because it obvious to us both that there was no going back.

After she moved to Atlanta I became the full-time, single dad to three adolescents entering their teen years. These were very difficult years. I was struggling to eke out an existence, keep an affordable roof over our heads, and provide for my children. At one point we crammed into a one bedroom loft sharing beds and one tiny bathroom. Eventually we upgraded to a small, two bedroom apartment and made the best of it. I continued to work every job conceivable, slowly working up from one bad job to a less bad job, to a not-so-bad job, to a promising job, and so on. It wasn't easy, but I was determined.

Coming out to my children was particularly tough for me. I'm not really sure why, but it was. I came out to my children twice but if you ask them they will each tell you their own memory of when they knew I was gay and none of their stories are the same nor match either of the times I thought I came out to them. The first time I came out to them they were in elementary and middle school. I sat them down one night and fumbled around with vague words and phrases. They sat staring at me with inquisitive looks on their faces. They knew I was trying to tell them something important, but I was doing a horrible job of communicating what that was. I don't recall what I said, but when I finished they seemed curiously satisfied and wanted to move on to watching a movie or whatever activity I had planned. *Well, that went really well!* I thought to myself. It wasn't many days afterward that I realized from comments they made that all of it went over their head. *Sigh. I'm going to have to do this all over again.*

The second time I came out to them was probably a year later. We were all lying in bed in my small one bedroom loft. It was the first apartment that was all mine after a series of renting rooms from friends while I tried to find my footing. I was proud of this old apartment above a hair salon in downtown Elkhart, Indiana. I shared my bed with whoever chose to sleep with me while the other two chose between the futon and the air mattress. Again, I don't recall what I said, but I knew I needed to be more specific and clear. This time I chose my words very intentionally. They listened intently and soberly. I could feel them processing the weight of what I had just told them. I asked if they had any questions. After a moment of silence, my daughter Annemarie said very tenderly and lovingly, "Dad, you know this doesn't make you a bad person." She had no idea how much I needed to hear those comforting and healing words.

From that moment on, I knew the important thing was that they felt loved, supported, and cared for by me, so that's what I focused on. Being a single dad of three teenagers required Herculean strength and stamina. I could barely make ends meet and often feared we were one week away from living in the homeless shelter.

One November day while managing The Daily Grind coffee shop, David walked into my life. I can still see him walking from the front door to the counter to order a hot chocolate. I was instantly smitten. I was certain I had seen every gay man in the South Bend area. But here was this beautiful man with a great sense of style and a endearing smile standing in front of me. I flirted, he returned the flirt and became a somewhat regular customer. The following February we went on our first date and the rest is romantic history. In 2021 we celebrated 15 years together. David came into my life fully aware of my struggles but loved me anyway. I have often referred to him as my BOFA (Breath Of Fresh Air). Our life together has been more than I could have ever hoped or dreamed for. David is the love of my life. Over the years, we have faced numerous extreme challenges together, but as he often reminds me, "Everything we do will either draw us closer together or push us farther apart." In light of that, we choose every step wisely.

It may appear to be an, "...and they all lived happily ever after," end to my story, but that is not at all the case. It has been years of hard work and intentional living. I had to confront it all and I had to know that God wasn't against me. I chose not to live as a victim or in my trauma. I stumbled a lot and I made some mistakes but never with the desire to hurt others. Sometimes what we need to do the most will hurt others we deeply love. I wish I could tell you I have perfect relationships with my former wife and children, but they aren't perfect. Relationships are never perfect because they involve flawed humans. What I do know is that at every twist and turn in my life I gave it my all. I sure know I was a damn good dad who did the best he could with what he had. I am a father who loves his children. I am a husband who is devoted to his husband. Most importantly, I am Joel and I now know who Joel is. I'm a man who isn't afraid to make bold moves.

"Life is a banquet, and most poor suckers are starving to death! LIVE!" - Auntie Mame

...*Now the tide is coming near*
I see the waves flowing
Out there on the ocean
I know my ship is coming in (coming in baby)
Just pass the horizon
And right where the sky ends
Cause out there on the ocean
Know my ship is coming in
But don't leave me hanging
I've been waiting too long
But this moment
My ship has finally come

—K'Jon, "On the Ocean"

ABOUT THE AUTHOR

As you can see, I know a little bit about making bold moves in life. Today I help people, organizations, and businesses make bold moves. I write and speak to audiences everywhere about the transformative power of living authentically not controlled by fear and shame. Life is too short to live any other way.

Visit JoelSpeaksOut.com and subscribe to keep up with my latest work, speaking appearances, and booking opportunities.

Life isn't perfect, but life is good. Now go live it!

ADDITIONAL PRAISE FOR GODLY... BUT GAY

"You told me that I was perfectly made in God's image, but when you found out I was gay, you told me I was broken and an abomination," Joel Barrett writes in this master class on sexuality and faith. This book is the most devastating yet hope-filled critique of the false promises of fundamentalist Christianity I've ever read. Period. It is a very important work because few people seem to understand that the most religiously fervent and godly people in America are gay. Joel is one such person, former pastor, father and husband. He has written a gem of a book on the human journey we all take-- whatever our sexual orientation or gender.

Frank Schaeffer, New York Times Bestselling author of, *Crazy For God*

The journey to live one's truth, starts with realizing you're not living your truth. Barrett rawly shares his compelling journey into the essence of his truth, inviting readers to embrace the power of themselves, to boldly live their lives on their terms, and to step out of the arena of living one's life based on others expectations. Instead, he invites them to live a life based on their relationship with God, not the contrived version that others have created of who God is and what he expects from us mortal humans.

Rick Clemons, Author, *Frankly My Dear I'm Gay*
Certified LGBTQ Life Coach

Anyone who has struggled with integrating their sexual identity into their daily lives will identify with Joel's story. His humorous and colorful account of his realization that he was gay is genuine and heartfelt. This book is a must read for anyone who has had their sexuality culturally repressed as well as anyone who is looking for a glimpse into the world of recovering from ultra-Christian indoctrination.

Kristen Thomas, Certified Sex Coach
Open The Doors Coaching

Godly but Gay…I recall the first occasion when I heard Joel utter the title of this book to me. At the time, he hadn't even written one word of his story down. I knew then that the world needed to hear this story, though. I am more convinced now. I believe that the world should get this kind of up-close, intimate look into the pain and suffering that is caused when we fundamentally believe that God loves everything about a person except for lov- ing the fact that they are attracted to the same sex.

I am grateful that Mr. Barrett has been vulnerable to put the details of his journey towards self-acceptance on the pages of a book. There are millions of Joel's and God made them just as God made all of us - in a godly image.

Dr. Nicole Price, Speaker, Trainer, Author
Lively Paradox

Like so many others coming from a traditional view of Christianity, Joel Barrett's story is one of hardship, struggle, and rejection. For years, he desperately sought a "cure" for his homosexuality only to find despair and hopelessness. In reality, he DIDN'T change. His new book peels back the mystery of how he journeyed through and finally found triumph and a new life filled with self-acceptance, love and true freedom. I highly recommend this book for anyone looking to embrace their true identity and find lasting peace.

John Paulk, OUT, proud gay man
Former Chairman of the Board,
Exodus International, North America
Former Director of the Homosexuality and Gender
Division of Focus on the Family and
Founder of the Love Won Out conference.

In Godly...But Gay, Joel Barrett bares his soul as he searches for love as he struggles to love himself. He travels the road where husband and preacher clash with the realization that he cannot run from being gay and having to face how to rebuild his life. One can feel the terror of facing yourself in the mirror in Joel's writing and yet finding redemption.

Dr. Marvin Curtis, Composer